SUCCESSFUL
SHOTGUN
SHOOTING

SUCCESSFUL SHOTGUN SHOOTING

Andrew A. Montague
with S. V. Beckwith

**Introduction by Lars Jacob,
The Orvis Company**

THE DERRYDALE PRESS
Lanham & New York

THE DERRYDALE PRESS

Published in the United States of America
by The Derrydale Press
4720 Boston Way, Lanham, Maryland 20706

Distributed by NATIONAL BOOK NETWORK

Library of Congress Cataloging-in-Publication Data

Montague, Andrew A.
    Successful shotgun shooting / Andrew A. Montague with
S. V. Beckwith ; foreword by Joseph A. Dearing.
      p. cm.
    Originally published: New York : Winchester Press, 1971.
    ISBN 1-56833-164-9 (pbk. : alk. paper)
    1. Shotguns. 2. Shooting. I. Beckwith, S. V. II. Title.

GV1179 .M6 2000
799.2"028'34 — dc21
                               00-031552

This Book Is Dedicated to My Wife
DOROTHY
My Companion in Life and Hunting
A. A. M.

ACKNOWLEDGMENTS

First, I would like to express my sincere thanks to "Uncle" Joe Dearing—outdoor editor, photographer and friend *par excellence*. Without his initial encouragement, this book would never have been started. I owe an even greater debt of gratitude to my friend and pupil S. V. Beckwith for undertaking the onerous task of getting my ideas down on paper. If the book succeeds in helping shooters to shoot better—as I hope it will—the credit will largely be due to "Beck's" long hours of questioning, clarifying and editing. And finally, I would like to thank Anne and Henry Eder for their patient and tireless assistance in making the instructional photographs which contribute so much to the book.

A.A.M.

CONTENTS

FOREWORD

Few people are as well qualified as Dr. Andrew A. Montague to write a book about shotgun shooting, and even fewer of those who possess such a wealth of knowledge and ability have ever done so. Dr. Montague began hunting in his native Hungary in 1923, bagging as many as 8,000 game birds on private preserves in a single year. At the same time, he participated in "driven bird" shoots for pheasants and partridges. From 1926 on he competed in trap and live bird shoots throughout Europe, winning such important individual shooting events as the world championship in Olympic trap, the Swiss trap and Hungarian trap and flyer championships.

Mark Arie, Olympic champion Jules Halasi, World champions Walter Warren and Francis Eisenlauer to name a few. I have also had the opportunity to hunt with some of the best game shots in Europe, where individual bags are often reckoned in the hundreds.

Each of these men has had his own individual way of shooting, a style which, used by him, had made him a champion; yet each style differed from the next. All had developed an effortless way of shooting that made it difficult to see just why they were so good, but certain fundamentals were always present.

I have no quarrel with any shooter's method that brings results. The figures on the score sheet and the birds in the bag are what count, and I have witnessed some fantastic shooting from many different positions. I believe, however, that the beginner should be taught certain fundamentals first, and the reasons for them, and only then be allowed to develop his own style within that framework.

With this in mind, the instructional part of this book is based not so much on my own personal way of shooting as on my observation of many experts and the additional experience accumulated during a fifteen-year affiliation with the gun department of Abercrombie & Fitch. I do not claim that my method is the "only one". However, I am sure that if you follow the guidelines set forth in this book you will succeed. You will acquire a sound basic stance, shooting position and technique on which to build, and all that will remain for you to do is to practice long and hard.

Good hunting to you!

ANDREW A. MONTAGUE

INTRODUCTION

Wingshooting, like golf or tennis, is a sport that can be taught. Proper form and technique combined with strong focus is the foundation of good shooting. *Successful Shotgun Shooting* is still the textbook of choice. Dr. Andrew Montague has taken the most important aspects of shooting and explains them in a way that is simple to understand and easy to perform. Whether you are a wingshooter or a clay enthusiast, whether you shoot sustained, swingthrough, or instinctive, Montague's book explains the foundation needed for them all.

For the beginner, Montague's explanation of the mechanics of a gun and the physics of a shot stream as it leaves the muzzle can only help in understanding what makes a better shot. The advanced shooter who has fallen into a slump will find refreshing reminders, like good shooting starts at the feet and not the muzzle of the gun.

Most of the technological advances made since this book was originally published are in shotgun shells. New shot cup designs, faster velocity, and the use of non-toxic shot can vary the opinion of choke constriction needed. Types of guns used and accessories have seen very little change. Dr. Montague's views on ethics and gun safety are based on good common sense and should be passed down from one generation of wingshooter to the next.

LARS JACOB
Manager, The Gun Department
The Orvis Company

PART ONE

How to Hit Moving Targets

CHAPTER 1

About Your Gun and How it Shoots

I like to start at the beginning. Thus readers who are already familiar with guns in general and shotguns in particular must bear with me for a page or two; the first part of this chapter is for the beginner.

In order to shoot a shotgun you need a gun and a shell.

The gun serves to hold the shell, fire it and, after it has been exploded, to channel the shot charge through the barrel in a straight line toward the target.

The barrel is a steel tube, generally from twenty-six to thirty inches long. It is of constant diameter except for the first two or three inches, where there is usually a slight constriction, and the last three or four inches, where it is slightly enlarged to accommodate the shell. The enlarged portion of the barrel which houses the shell is called the "chamber" and the constriction at the muzzle end is known as the "choke." The choke regulates the circumference of the shot pattern, much as an adjustable nozzle controls the spray of water from a garden hose.

To insure that the force of the explosion exerts itself only forward, the rear end of the barrel is sealed off by the breech, which contains the firing mechanism and the bolting system.

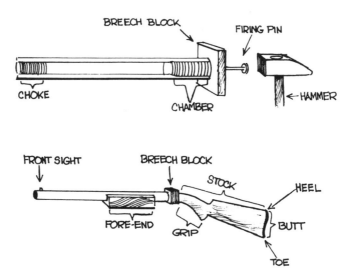

Since it would hardly be possible to hold a naked steel tube in your hand and aim it with any degree of accuracy, the barrel and firing mechanism are attached to a piece of wood called the "stock." The stock is shaped so that its rear end ("butt") can rest against

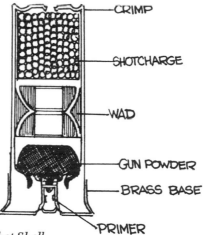

CRIMP

SHOTCHARGE

WAD

GUN POWDER

BRASS BASE

PRIMER

Cross-Section of a Modern Shot Shell.

your shoulder and, extending forward and slightly upward, support the breech end of the barrel at the level of your eye. It has a place shaped to accommodate your right hand, called the "grip," and is accompanied by a second piece, fitted beneath the barrel for your left hand to grasp, which is called the "fore-end."

The shell is a cylindrical container of paper or plastic with a metal base. It is loaded with a primer, gunpowder, wad and shot. The shot charge consists of spherical lead pellets, of which there are usually several hundred in a hunting load. Pulling the gun's trigger releases a hammer which hits the firing pin, detonating the primer. This in turn ignites the powder, causing it to explode. The explosive force, being contained laterally by the barrel walls and at the rear of the barrel by the breech block, can react in one direction only — toward the open or muzzle end of the barrel. The explosion's force pushes the wad forward, which drives the shot charge ahead and through the barrel with enough momentum to continue to a distant target.

19

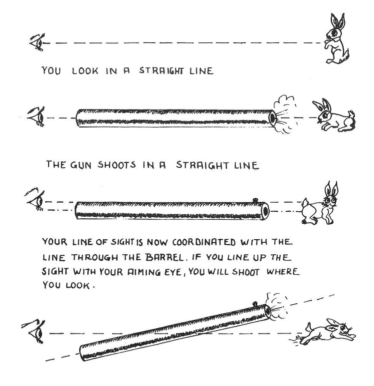

YOU LOOK IN A STRAIGHT LINE

THE GUN SHOOTS IN A STRAIGHT LINE

YOUR LINE OF SIGHT IS NOW COORDINATED WITH THE LINE THROUGH THE BARREL. IF YOU LINE UP THE SIGHT WITH YOUR AIMING EYE, YOU WILL SHOOT WHERE YOU LOOK.

IF YOU MOVE THE GUN OUT OF THE LINE OF SIGHT WHILE YOU ARE LOOKING AT THE TARGET, THE GUN WILL SHOOT ONE WAY WHILE YOU LOOK ANOTHER.

BASIC THEORY OF SHOOTING

To hit a target you must see it, and you can look only in a straight line. Shotguns, within their effective range limits, propel shot in a straight line, too. Therefore, if you can coordinate your line of vision from eye to target with the line along which the barrel directs the shot, you will hit what you are looking at. In other words, if you could look at the target through the barrel of your gun while firing it, you would score a hit, provided the target remained stationary and was within range.

20

Since you cannot look through the barrel, gun makers have provided a substitute: a bead on top of the front end of the barrel, which is called the "front sight." If you look along the top of the barrel so that all you see is the bead, you will get the same result as if you were looking down the bore — your line of sight will be coordinated with the line through the barrel. Therefore, *if you line up the front sight with your aiming eye, you will shoot where you look.* This is the basic principle of shotgun shooting.

If either the gun or your aiming eye moves out of this all-important coordinated position, you will look in one direction but the gun will shoot in another. Remember this throughout your shooting career: *always look with the gun.*

CHAPTER 2

Proper Shooting Position

How does one get into the *lined-up position* which enables him to *look with the gun?* The best way is to learn the correct sequence of movements, and then practice them with an empty gun, over and over *and over* again, until the separate movements blend together and the whole procedure becomes second nature. The easiest way to assume the proper shooting position is as follows:

To begin, stand with your feet eight to ten inches apart, holding the gun by its grip with the right hand alone, the barrel pointing straight up. Next, put all your weight on your left foot while holding in your left hip.

Taking a correct shooting position: Weight has been transferred to the left foot, and the right foot drawn in close; the left hand is at eye level, the palm up and open; the head is tilted slightly forward, and the right hand is about to place the gun's fore-end in the left palm.

This may cause your right heel to leave the ground. Bring the right foot forward just enough to permit the heel to drop again, so that the whole foot is on the ground but without any weight on it.

Now tilt your head slightly forward, and advance it until your chin is even with your left toes. Raise your empty left hand to eye level, the palm up and open, and almost simultaneously, raise the gun until the heel of the stock is near the center of your chest (see photograph). Then drop the barrel, placing the fore-end in the palm of your left hand. *Still keeping your head in*

The lined-up shooting position: Weight is solidly on the left foot; right foot is on the ground but has little or no weight on it. Note the short distance between the feet. The right shoulder, hunched forward, cradles the entire butt surface. Head is tilted forward. Left hand is far enough forward to place a lot of gun between hands and body, affording good control.

position, lift the stock until your cheek rests against the comb, and draw the gun back until the butt contacts your shoulder. If you have done all this correctly (and if your gun fits you properly, of which more later) the front sight will now be aligned with your aiming eye, and the line through the barrel will be coordinated with your line of sight. From here on in, you can *look with the gun and it will shoot where you look.*

24

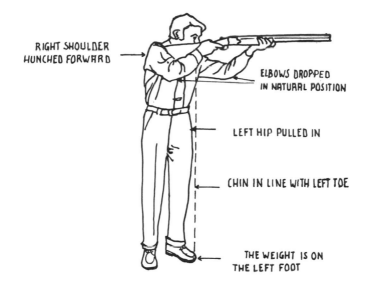

RIGHT SHOULDER
HUNCHED FORWARD →

ELBOWS DROPPED
IN NATURAL POSITION

LEFT HIP PULLED IN

CHIN IN LINE WITH LEFT TOE

THE WEIGHT IS ON
THE LEFT FOOT

Of course, once the gun is in this lined-up position your head, shoulders and arms must remain fixed and may not move independently of each other: *your upper body and the gun must move as a single unit when tracking a moving target.* Since your feet should not move either, your body turn must be accomplished by your waist and hips, as if the two halves of your body were connected by a universal joint.

There are good reasons for every element of this shooting position. The upper portion of the body, in its fixed or "lined-up" position, keeps the gun aligned at all times, while the lower portion provides the mobility needed to follow a moving target. Thus proper placing of the feet, distribution of weight, and balance are just as important as proper gun mounting. Now let us consider some of the gun-mounting details.

The right-hand grip. All fingers have a firm grasp, and the thumb is on the left side. The exact position of the hand is determined by the length of the trigger finger, for only the first segment is used to pull the trigger. Using the second segment would place the middle finger too close to the trigger guard, where it would get bruised when the gun recoils.

The right hand holds the gun at the grip. It should be positioned so that you can easily pull the trigger with the first segment of your index finger, which is your trigger finger. Always remember, however, that *the trigger finger should never be placed inside the trigger guard or on the trigger until actually shooting.* This finger should be held along the outer edge of the guard where it can be moved easily to the shooting position as the gun is mounted. You should practice this movement until it becomes automatic: gun on shoulder, finger on trigger; gun off shoulder, finger on the guard. Leaving the finger inside the guard when not shooting can only lead to accidents.

Once the right hand has been correctly positioned, it should remain in place whenever the gun is carried or held by the grip. If the hand must be repositioned before you shoot, you will lose precious time. All fingers hold the grip firmly, with the thumb on the left side as in gripping a tennis racquet.

Shotgun triggers are not squeezed off, they are pulled; you have no time to complete a long squeeze,

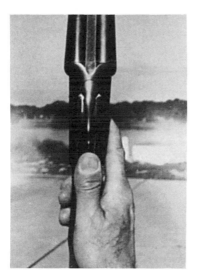

How to split your thumb! After sliding the safety forward, be sure to move your thumb back to the left side of the grip for a shot. Many thumbs have been cut when left in the position shown above.

as when shooting a rifle. However, a very slight amount of pressure should be exerted in first contacting the trigger in order to make the final pull instantaneous. This speed takes on special importance in competitive shooting. Loose or sloppy trigger handling will cause your timing to vary.

As you hold the gun at the grip be certain to leave some room between the trigger guard and your middle finger. This is important, for many a middle finger has been bruised by the recoil driving the guard into it. (Bruised middle or trigger fingers of the right hand can also be caused by too short a stock. When you buy a gun the stock should be adjusted to the proper length for you by adding a rubber or lace-on recoil pad or spacers, or cutting off a slice of the butt as the case may be. This subject is discussed in detail in Chapter 11.)

Just as important is the position of your thumb. It should be on the left side of the grip, never on top. I have seen many thumbs cut badly by the top lever of a shotgun. In addition, positioning the thumb to the left gives a firmer hold.

Front view of the lined-up position: Both elbows are in a relaxed position away from the body—the right not high enough to cause strain, yet low enough to afford sufficient leverage to prevent the gun from jumping when fired; the left, sufficiently low to permit the hand to support the fore-end comfortably.

The right elbow should be in an easy position away from your body — not high enough to cause any strain in holding it there and low enough to give leverage to the hand and thus prevent the gun from jumping when fired. Note also that a high right elbow tends to cant the gun.

The left hand grasps the fore-end as far out as it comfortably can, so that the arm is extended, but without locking the elbow. After all, the gun constitutes an inert weight extending beyond your reach, and the more of it you can place between your left hand and your body, the better will be your control — the easier it will be to start your swing, and to follow the course of a target should it change direction.

It is important to have your left hand at eye level. This hand is a pivot point and if it is higher or lower

28

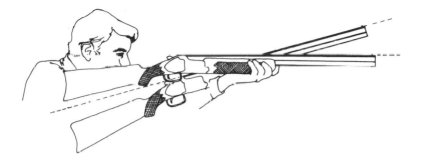

The left hand is a pivot point and if it is higher or lower than eye level the gun will not line up with your line of sight.

than eye level, the gun will not line up with your line of sight. This will tend to make you inaccurate and will also waste precious time as you lift or lower the muzzle to its proper position.

The correct position of the left hand is easy to assume if the gun can be preaimed, as in shooting trap. You can take as much time as you need to adjust it. In the field, however, this hand must be quickly raised to its shooting position and adjusted enroute. This is done by relaxing your grip enough for it to act as a channel through which the fore-end can slide as the right hand brings the butt to your shoulder. The left hand should not grasp the fore-end firmly until the gun has reached the shooting position. If the fore-end is gripped firmly too far out, the butt may not have room to clear your armpit or clothing as the right hand raises it to position.

The left elbow should drop into a comfortable position. It should never be raised high. After all, the left arm is supporting part of the gun's weight and it is much easier to push such a weight up from beneath than to lift it from the side.

The right shoulder comes last in this analysis because placing the gun against it is the last move in assuming the shooting position. Proper positioning of the butt against the shoulder is one of the most important acts leading to consistently good shooting.

When mounting the gun, hunch your right shoulder forward as if you were about to push a heavy weight, for this is exactly what will occur when the gun is fired and you must counteract the recoil. Raise the gun as previously described and holding it firmly, pull it back into the cradle formed by the hunched right shoulder. This pulling force should be positive enough for you to feel the pressure of the gun against your shoulder, but without tensing any muscles. If the gun is held in this manner, the backward force of the recoil will push against you, but if it is held away from the shoulder or held too loosely, this force will cause the gun to gain momentum and to hit instead of push. It is much easier to roll with a punch than to take a hit.

Remember that the position of the left hand and the position of the cheekbone will determine the correct position of the butt against your shoulder. It is important, therefore, that your left hand be at eye level and that your head be tilted forward before you raise the butt to your shoulder. The left hand is a pivot point and if it is higher or lower than eye level the gun will not line up with your line of sight and you will lose time in raising or lowering the muzzle to its proper position. Your gun mounting will also be inconsistent.

The oval-shaped butt must rest with its entire surface against the shoulder. When the force of the recoil is distributed over all of the butt, the shock will be felt less than if it is concentrated in one part. Faulty positioning of the butt can result not only in a bruised shoulder and arm, and sometimes headaches, but also in erratic shooting.

Correct positioning of the butt against the shoulder. Note that the stock does not project above the shoulder, and the butt is positioned well in from the shoulder joint, not out on the biceps.

31

ONE EYE, OR TWO?

The only aspect of shooting position we have not yet discussed is whether both eyes, or only the aiming eye should be open. The statement is often made that "you should always shoot a shotgun with both eyes open" but if you ask why, you rarely get more than a shocked, reproachful stare for having dared to question so hallowed a precept.

The truth is that you can shoot as well with one eye as with two. Except for a few incoming shots, the second eye only helps to judge distance, like the range finder on your camera. To snap the picture, all you need is one eye. Even with shooters who use both eyes, at the final split second before firing the master eye takes control. The other eye "looks" but does not necessarily "see."

If you are right-handed and your right eye is the master eye, all is well. You can keep both eyes open if you wish. On the other hand, if your left eye is the master and you mount the gun right-handed, you will invariably cross-fire. In other words, instead of sighting along the barrel with your lined-up right eye, you will align the front end of the barrel with your left eye. This will give you an automatic lead to the left that you do not visualize. While you will hit many targets going to the left, you will shoot far behind those going to the right.

This brings us to the critical question, how can you tell your master eye? It is really quite simple to determine this. Take a piece of cardboard approximately eight inches square and punch a one-quarter-inch round hole in the middle. Hold the card in your right hand and

How cross-firing occurs. If your left eye is your master eye and you mount the gun right-handed, you'll tend to align the muzzle with your left eye as you place the stock against your right shoulder. The gun will then point (and shoot) to the left.

lower it in front of you. Now choose a target some distance away. Without moving your eyes from this object, lift the card with outstretched arm and, with both eyes open, look through the hole at the target. Then close your right eye. If you lose the target you can be sure that the right eye is your master eye. The same applies to your left eye. If you keep seeing the target through the hole with your right eye closed, you are "left-eyed" and had better shoot with only one eye open, or change to left-handed gun mounting.

An even simpler way to determine your master eye is to point a finger at a distant object while keeping both eyes open. Then close your right eye. If the finger jumps to the right, out of line with the object, you can be sure the right eye is your master eye. The reverse applies to your left eye. If you keep seeing the object over your finger when the right eye is closed, you are "left-eyed." Incidentally, some shooters, particularly older ones, are right-eyed when they are fresh, but become prone to cross-firing when they get tired. This is worth thinking about if you hit a string of inexplicable misses.

33

CHAPTER **3**

Safety

Before we proceed from "dry" practice to actual shooting practice, using live ammunition, we must take a long, hard look at the subject of safety. *No excuse can ever justify the careless handling of a gun.* Ninety-nine per cent of all shooting accidents are caused by carelessness, thoughtlessness or downright laziness. And tardy regret, regardless of how deeply felt, is of no use to the victim who has lost life or limb.

Exclamations such as "I was sure it was unloaded" — "I was sure he was behind me" — "I thought the safety was on" are as helpful as an umbrella after the rain. A little forethought, such as checking a gun to make sure it is unloaded and keeping constantly aware of your hunting companions' whereabouts, can save a life, a limb or an eye.

In my business I have witnessed and heard of many so-called shooting accidents, most of which could have been avoided through common-sense gun handling. It should be evident to anyone that the charge comes from the muzzle end of a gun, and that this end is the one to watch. Never point it toward yourself or anyone else, whether the gun is loaded or not. Never, under any circumstances, leave a loaded gun leaning against a fence, tree, bush or side of a building. More than once I have seen a gun that had been placed "securely" against a wire fence fall to the ground and go off. It only takes a few seconds to unload a shotgun, regardless of what type it is, and every hunter owes it to himself and his companions to do just that at the time it should be done. The seconds required may save someone a lot of grief.

Don't tolerate anyone pointing a gun at you, loaded or unloaded, accidentally or otherwise. I have seen an "experienced" hunter with a gun cradled in his arm turn and, sweeping the gun in an arc, point it at all his hunting partners. The fact that he had never shot anyone during the thirty years he had been hunting didn't mean that he might not accidentally shoot some-one in the next thirty seconds. Don't be polite. Tell such a careless person never to point his gun in your direction again. It may prevent your being shot at and teach the errant one a bit of gun safety at the same time.

I recall an experience while hunting with a dis-

How not to carry a gun.

Two more unsafe gun carries.

36

Safer ways of carrying a gun. In the stance on the right, the shooter already has the right hand in correct position and could assume shooting position quite readily. This is a practical carrying position when there is some possibility of birds getting up.

tinguished gentleman many years my senior. He had the disturbing habit of allowing his gun to point at his companion. I stood it as long as I could and finally asked him to point the gun anywhere except at me. He was very upset and offended, and assured me that his gun was unloaded. To prove his point, he opened his double and, to his astonishment and great embarrassment, revealed two live shells in the chambers.

Maybe it isn't loaded—but don't do it, anyway.

Don't get in or out of cars with loaded guns, and never grasp a gun with the muzzle pointed toward you while putting it in a car or taking it from someone.

Don't sit, leaning your chin on the muzzle.

Never keep a loaded gun in the house, even in some inaccessible place "where the kids won't find it." They will find it anyway. Teach your children to respect guns and don't hesitate to punish them if you catch them pointing even a toy gun at someone. I can still remember the licking I received when I was about four years old for pointing a popgun at a playmate. Although it happened fifty-some years ago, it has kept me watching the muzzles of my guns ever since. Finally, never pick up a gun from a rack, or accept one from someone else, without breaking it or clearing the action to insure that it is unloaded.

This way of relaxing with a gun always makes me shudder.

LOADING AND UNLOADING

Break-open guns, the side-by-sides and over-and-unders, are the easiest to load and unload. To break the gun, grasp the fore-end with your left hand, tilt the top of the gun away from you, and steady the stock between your right forearm and your body. In this position you have "a hold" on the stock and better leverage for your thumb to push on the top lever. Do not pull on the barrels until the top lever has been pushed completely over; the locking mechanism must clear the barrels before the gun can be broken. When closing the gun, do not hold your thumb against the top lever. Snap it shut with moderate force and let the lever "go home." The gun was made to snap and if it is not closed all the way, you put a strain on the locking mechanism and may cause a misfire.

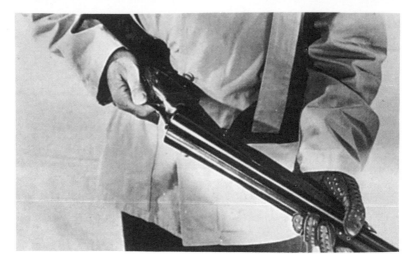

The best way to open any break-open action. Wedge the stock between your forearm and body, push down on the top lever, and only then start pulling on the barrels. It's like opening a door; you don't push until you have turned the knob.

The side-by-side is a little easier to load than the over-and-under. This is because the latter must be broken to a slightly greater angle and it is a bit more difficult to put a shell in the bottom barrel. However, the difference between the two is so slight as to be of no great importance.

When closing a gun, especially those without automatic safeties, *be sure never to have any fingers inside the trigger guard.* This should be obvious, but beginners still do it.

There are times, with a double-barrel gun, when you badly need a third or even a fourth shot. A very fast third can be fired if you learn to hold a shell between the index and middle fingers of your left hand, provided your gun has an automatic ejector to throw out the empties. In this situation, with an over-and-under, the selector should be set to fire the top barrel first since it is the easier one to load with the third shell.

40

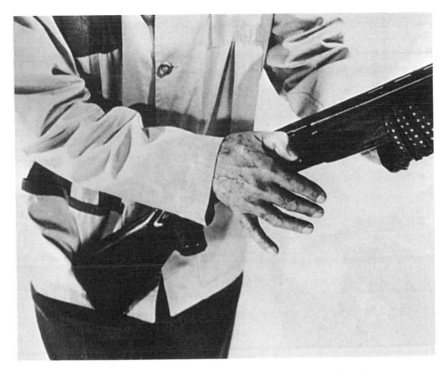

To open an automatic, brace the butt against your right thigh and pull back quickly on the bolt with your thumb.

The same technique can be used with two shells, holding them between fingers of the left hand. I was never able to hold two satisfactorily but some of my companions became artists at this trick and could get off four shots nearly as fast as with an automatic.

When loading an automatic, keep your fingers out of the loading slot. There is no need to guide the first shell into the chamber. Just drop it in the slot and push the release button. The mechanism will do the rest.

41

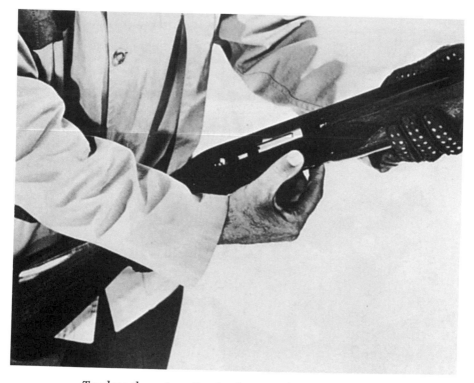

To close the automatic, simply press the release button with your right thumb and be sure to keep your fingers well away from the action port. Never try to ease the forward movement of the bolt.

When closing your automatic, don't hang onto the bolt handle. You are not "saving" the gun; you are just asking for a misfire. So let it snap home. The bolt you are trying to close so gently will soon ram itself back and forth with lightning speed on your second shell. It is made for such work, so don't worry. Also, when pushing the release button, do it with your right thumb and with no fingers on the slot side. This insures against any nasty cuts or bruises from the closing bolt.

The procedures for loading and unloading pump guns are quite similar to those for automatics. When unloading either of them, be sure there are no shells left in the magazine. Working the bolt or action slide is not enough. The gun should be turned so you can look in the magazine. For safety, the action of these guns should remain open when not actually hunting.

Regardless of the kind of gun you use, *the safety should always be on when loading or unloading*, and the gun should never be pointed in anyone's direction. Many coaches insist that the safety should only be released as part of the act of gun-mounting and this is a desirable practice. However, safeties are fallible, and there's no such thing as a loaded gun that's safe — there are only shooters who have developed sound safety habits. The simpliest and best procedure is to *treat every gun like a loaded gun.*

CHAPTER **4**

Shooting at Moving Targets

Now at last you can start shooting.
Ideally, the place to begin is on a skeet field, provided
that you can obtain exclusive use of it. As a practical
matter, however, this is not always possible, and it's
certainly not wise to start out as a member of a regular
skeet squad — this can be very confusing for the beginner, with advice coming from all sides. So if you do
not have exclusive use of the field, or if none is available,
you should begin with a hand trap or practice trap,
using them to duplicate the skeet-field situations described below.

The correct way to use a hand trap. The thrower should always stand a step behind the shooter, and to his right.

There are several types of hand traps, the Western being perhaps the simplest to operate, and with practice, all kinds of targets can be thrown with them in any direction. A word of caution, however: The thrower should always stand a foot or two behind the shooter, and to his *right*. These traps are made for right-handed throwers and if a target slides out of the trap prematurely, or breaks in it, the shooter can be hit if he is on the wrong side.

A safe way to practice incoming targets.

For crossing targets and incomers, the thrower must be well protected from flying shot. Perhaps the easiest protection to be found will be a high bank, with the thrower standing on top and the shooter below, but so positioned that neither can see the other. Even when so protected, the thrower should wear shooting glasses to protect his eyes from possible ricocheting pellets.

A bit more expensive than hand traps are the so-called practice traps. These are the same in principle as the regular traps used on skeet and trap fields, but simpler in construction. They must be cocked manually and released by foot or hand pressure. One advantage to these traps is that the shooter can operate them alone, and some models will also throw doubles, though adjustments for height and angle of flight are somewhat limited. If the trap is operated by an assistant, the shooter should protect himself by standing to the left as in using hand traps.

46

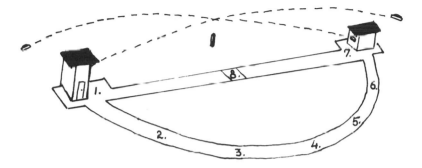

Layout of a skeet field showing station numbers and high and low houses.

The best targets to start shooting at are those that require practically no lead — those going away from you at about eye level or a little higher. On a skeet field these will be found at station 7 with low house birds.

Assume the shooting position, with the gun lined up over the marker post behind station 8 that indicates the crossing point over which all targets fly. Take all the time you need to get your shooting position perfect. Later on you can practice calling for the bird from the ready position described in the next chapter but for now, mount the gun before you call for the bird. Call for the bird and remember to swing from the hips, up or down as needed but keeping your head, shoulders and arms in the fixed or lined-up position. As soon as the target comes in your line of sight, pull the trigger but *keep on swinging*. Since you are "pre-aimed" in the lined-up position, you will hit the target provided you have not lifted your head or moved the gun out of position.

47

Shoot at these easy straightaway targets until you can hit them consistently and are quite familiar with proper gun mounting. It is a good idea to shoot no more than twenty-five shells the first few practice sessions, and to pause between each five shots. Your ability to concentrate will be limited at first, and your muscles will not be used to this new exercise. Both mind and muscles must be conditioned gradually, for it takes time to bring them to top effectiveness.

Once you have the feel for outgoing targets, you should try your hand at incomers. This too can best be done at station 7 on a skeet field, but with targets from the high house. Line up the gun over the marker post and then swing back to the high house. Point your gun under the opening, as this will let you see the target as soon as it emerges. Call for the target, swing with it, and pull the trigger while still swinging. Don't let the target come in too close before shooting because the nearer it is when you pull the trigger, the smaller will be the shot pattern. Also, if you let the target get too close, it may go past the area in which you can swing most easily.

Again, if you keep yourself lined up and do not move out of your lined-up position, all you need to do is keep looking at the target, follow through, and you will score a hit.

Once you are hitting both incomers and straight-aways with reasonable consistency, you can start working on targets that require a lead, which are known as crossing targets. Before you start shooting at them, however, you should understand what "lead" means. A shot charge takes a fraction of a second to go from gun

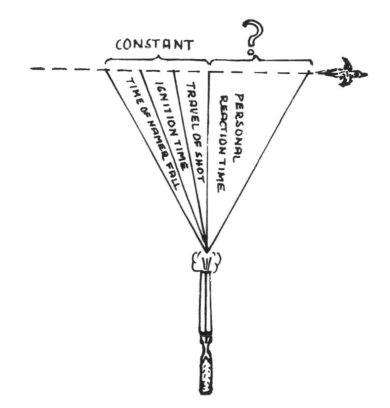

The component elements of the time lag which makes it necessary to lead a crossing target.

muzzle to target and the command impulse from brain to trigger finger requires another fraction. In addition, it takes time for the firing mechanism to function, from trigger pull to muzzle blast. These factors create enough of a time lag so that if you point your gun squarely at a target moving at right angles without compensating for the time lag, you will invariably shoot behind it. Therefore *you must shoot where the target is going to be when the shot charge reaches it*. This requires you to shoot ahead of the target, or to lead it.

49

How much you should lead a target depends on its speed, distance from you, and the angle of its flight. The faster the target, the more nearly it approaches a right angle in crossing, and the farther it is from you, the more you must lead it. It is a fallacy, however, to quote specific leads. Speed of target, live or artificial, and speed of shot can easily be calculated, but reaction time is highly individual. The lead for a specific target might be one foot for one person and three feet for someone else with slower wiring of the nerves. It is a good rule of thumb, though, if you miss a crossing target, to increase your lead, as the great majority of these targets are missed behind.

If you overlead a target, the "stringing" of the shot pattern may still give you a hit. The shot charge flies in somewhat of an elliptical cone, strung out to a considerable length, so even if the leading pellets are well ahead of the target, there is still a chance for some of those following to score a hit. On the other hand, if the leading pellets are behind the target, the others will be even farther back.

Following a crossing target and adjusting to the proper lead while swinging require maximum control of your gun and ease of swing. These are obtained by properly positioning both the upper and lower parts of your body, as previously explained, and making sure that your movements are relaxed and free from tension. It is important for your weight to be entirely on your left foot because most of the swing is executed as a pivot around the left leg. Only in the last quarter of an extreme right swing does your weight shift gradually a bit to the right foot. Balance is the determining factor in this.

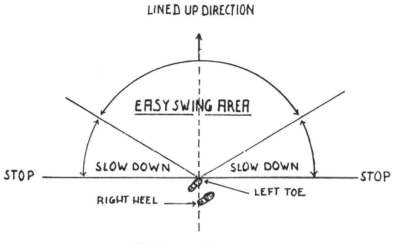

LINED UP DIRECTION

EASY SWING AREA

STOP

SLOW DOWN

SLOW DOWN

STOP

RIGHT HEEL

LEFT TOE

The horizontal swing area.

In the correct shooting position, with the gun properly lined up, you will find that it points over an imaginary line drawn from your right heel though your left big toe. You will find also, when positioned correctly, that you can turn (swing) ninety degrees to the left and ninety degrees to the right without changing the position of your feet, thus giving you a swing area of one-half a complete circle.

On the left and right ends of the swing, you have to stop. And before you stop completely, you slow down, in the last thirty degrees on each side. You do not slow down in the middle hundred and twenty degrees and this I call the *"easy swing area."*

51

The normal shooting position.

All targets should be shot at in the easy swing area, as this is where you have full control over the gun and can adjust your lead to follow targets should they change course. If a crossing target runs out of the easy swing area, you will have to slow down or even stop and this will cause you to shoot behind it. And any time you stop your swing before or just as you pull the trigger on a crossing target, you will miss behind it. *Always follow through with your swing* after pulling the trigger to be sure you do not stop too soon. The follow-through is especially important when you need a second shot for then it becomes a continuation of the original swing and you need not start the gun again.

The Horizontal Swing.

Note that from the normal shooting position (opposite page) you can turn 90 degrees both to the left and right without changing the position of your feet. However, at the extreme limits of the swing area the stance becomes somewhat strained, and your swing will tend to slow down.

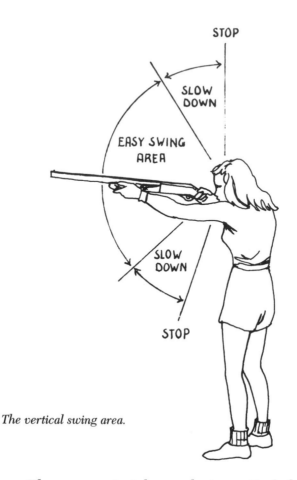

STOP

SLOW DOWN

EASY SWING AREA

SLOW DOWN

STOP

The vertical swing area.

The same principles apply to vertical shots. You will note that by bending forward from the waist, you can point at a spot just a few yards in front of your feet, and that by bending back and placing all your weight on the right foot, you can point the gun straight up. At this point, however, you have to stop. This is the upper end of your vertical swing area and you will slow down before reaching it. You should, therefore, shoot at incoming targets before they reach about twenty-five degrees from the top of the swing area.

The Vertical Swing.

It is possible to point the gun just a few yards in front of your feet, and it is also possible, by putting your weight on the right foot and bending back, to swing the gun straight up. Whenever possible, however, avoid shooting in the extreme positions.

With this knowledge of leads and swing areas, it is time now to shoot at crossing targets. Stand at station 6 on a skeet field and try your hand at incoming, or high house, birds. You want to shoot at these in the easy swing area, so line up the gun for the marker post, or a little to its right, and swing back, winding up your body, as it were, to the high house. Point the gun below the opening and call for the bird. Swing with it and through it, since it must be led, and when you have the proper lead, pull the trigger. Again, the proper lead depends on the individual, but, in my experience, most people find that a foot is about right. Try it and see how much you need.

You should now do the same thing with low house birds. This time, however, start at station 2, line up a little to the left of the marker and then swing over to the low house. The lead for this shot is the same as for a high house bird at station 6.

From here you can go to the middle stations where you will find that, in order to hit the targets, you must increase your leads considerably. You will have to learn exactly how much for yourself, since nobody can provide a general prescription for leading which can be applied to everyone. As we have said, individual mental and physical reaction times vary too widely to permit definite rules to be given.

COMMON SHOOTING MISTAKES

Most shooters are convinced that most of their misses come from using the wrong lead. Sometimes they are right, of course, but often I feel that too much emphasis is put on leading, and not enough on keeping the gun moving. Actually, no lead is really necessary for many of your shots. A good portion of your hunting shots, for example, are at birds going away from you. In the United States this is particularly true of walked-up quail, pheasant and partridge. A further considerable number of shots are taken as incomers, and so the number of true crossing shots is in the minority. The narrow quartering angle of most straightaway and in coming targets makes leads practically unnecessary, since the shot pattern is wide enough to compensate for the slight lead required. In such cases you will always bag your bird if you maintain your lined-up position *and do not stop your swing as you pull the trigger.*

In my experience, most misses are caused not by insufficient lead, but by stopping the gun as the shot is made or just pointing it at the target without swinging at all — in other words, spot shooting. Always continue to track the bird until you see it fall. Many of the best shots are not aware of leading even crossing birds at all, but they all have a moving gun when they pull the trigger, and they keep it moving well after the shot has been made.

Another mistake which is not given enough attention is shooting out of range. Don't forget that the normal effective shotgun range is only 40 yards. Of course, magnum shells and large shot can stretch it out 15 to 25 yards more, but at those ranges even the experts find it difficult to judge leads, and nothing is more irresponsible than to shoot at game beyond the effective range of your gun or shooting skill. Shooting out of range not only cripples birds and causes unnecessary

Never lift your head as you shoot. If you raise it from the shooting position the gun will shoot in one direction while you look in another. Always look with the gun.

suffering, but also ruins hunting for the next fellow, who might have had a decent shot if you had not driven the bird away.

Lifting your head is still another common cause of missing. This can occur either at the instant of firing, or earlier in looking for the target. In either case, the coordination between your line of sight and the line through the barrel is broken, and you look in one direction while the gun shoots in another. Remember always to look with the gun.

Lifting your head can sometimes be blamed on poorly fitted shooting glasses which make you lift your head in order to see through the center of the lenses. It is important that the lens and not the frame be in your line of vision when your head is down in the shooting position, and most regular shooting glasses are made this way.

Closing both eyes, or flinching, is a common fault with beginners. Fear of the noise, blast or recoil when the trigger is pulled can cause this reaction. It is usually accompanied by a jerking of the gun which, of course, results in a miss. Be sure you are looking at the target when you pull the trigger — it is hard to score a hit with both eyes closed! Lots of dry practice, with a dummy "snap cap" to protect your gun's firing pin, is the best cure for this.

Cross firing occurs when your left eye is the master eye and you keep both eyes open. The easiest way to remedy this is to close or squint your left eye when shooting. Should you have trouble in squinting, you can apply a so-called "cross-firing segment" to your shooting glasses. Plain sunglasses will do, provided the upper part of the rim does not interfere with your vision when your head is tilted forward to get down on the gun.

The application of this cross-firing segment is very simple. Take a small piece of surgical tape, or Band-Aid, ⅜" x 1". Put on your glasses and sight your gun in the proper lined-up position. Then have someone place the tape on the left lens at a slight angle, higher on the inside, so that it blocks out the vision of your left eye (see illustration). This is easily checked: if you cannot see the target when you close your right eye, the tape is in the correct place.

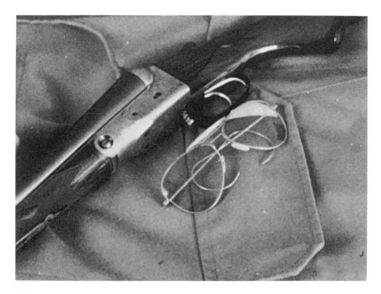

Shooting glasses with cross-firing segment in place. When your head is normally upright your vision will not be obstructed, but when you tilt it forward into shooting position, the vision of your left eye will automatically be blocked out.

You will notice that if you lift your head off the gun and let it assume the normal upright position, this small patch on your glasses will not obstruct your vision. Thus you can see with both eyes and judge distance right up to the moment when you actually "come down" on the gun to shoot.

A canted gun can't shoot where you look.

Tilting or canting the gun occurs when it is not positioned properly on the shoulder. This may be caused by a wrong fit or by your lifting the right elbow too high. A look at the illustration will show you that the gun will not shoot where you look, especially the lower barrel of an over-and-under, and both barrels of a side-by-side.

The remedy is to have a center bead mounted on the rib; any canting will throw this little bead out of alignment, to one side or the other.

61

Never push out your left hip. Doing so restricts your movement and reduces both the vertical and the horizontal easy-swing areas. This shooter's left hand is also too far forward.

Pushing the left hip out is the most frequent error made by the ladies. It seems to be a natural movement on their part — I have found it with about ninety percent of my female students. This fault should be watched carefully and overcome. It not only restricts your swing area but also, because you are not leaning into the gun, can cause bad recoil troubles.

Keep your base narrow, and never stand with your right foot on tiptoe. Too wide a base limits your swing area, and the tiptoe stance is unstable.

Wrong stance: If you stand with your feet too far apart you can never get your weight on the left foot as you should. This will restrict all your movements and considerably reduce your swing area. And since you are not leaning into the gun, the recoil will push you back, thus delaying your second shot and making it uncertain. Ignore the usual advice to flex your left knee. Flexion here is unnecessary, and a hinged position can lead to error. Finally, remember never to stand with your right foot on tiptoe. While there should be no weight on this foot, it should, nevertheless, be on the ground. Place it as close to the left foot as may be necessary to keep it on the ground. *Correct footwork is essential to good shooting.*

63

CHAPTER 5

Shooting at Game

Up to now we have been concerned with shooting at inanimate targets, with the gun already mounted in the lined-up position. When hunting, however, you cannot expect a flushed bird to wait while you get ready to shoot at it. Thus you must learn to assume a position in which you are *ready* to mount the gun with a minimum of delay. In field shooting you are always fighting for time, and the "ready position" is an intermediate position designed to save you as much time as possible in assuming the shooting position. To accomplish this, the ready position pre-aims your body so that all that remains for you to do is to swing with the

The Ready Position. The body is in the shooting position, but the gun has not been mounted; instead of being against the shoulder, the butt is near the middle of the chest with the toe turned slightly to the right. However, the head is already tilted forward, the left hand at eye level, the weight shifted to the left foot, and the right shoulder is hunched forward ready to receive the butt.

bird's flight, put the gun to your shoulder, and shoot. You will find that when the gun comes up, it will point where you are looking, namely, at the target. Thereafter, all you need to do is keep swinging and, when you have the proper lead, pull the trigger.

The easiest way to describe the ready position is to work backwards, so first place yourself in the lined-up position. Then, without moving your head or changing the position of your elbows, turn the gun with your right wrist and drop the stock so that the heel touches the bottom of your rib cage, just right of center, with the toe pointing at a slight angle to the right. Since your left elbow remains stationary, the left hand stays at eye level, but it turns just a bit in response to the rotation of the right hand. You are now in the ready position.

How to change stance. If birds get up to the right of your easy-swing area, you should change your stance by taking a small step with your left foot, and mount the gun only in the last split-second as you complete the turn.

In the ready position you will notice that, except for the slight turn of the wrists, you are also in the shooting position. The head, shoulders and arms are in place for shooting, ready to receive the gun. In a fraction of a second you can give it a turn with your wrists and move it back to your shoulder, lined up perfectly. No time has been lost in shoving the gun forward, raising it up, or in getting your head down. This is the fastest way I know of bringing a shotgun into the shooting position.

Fast and accurate shooting depends on what you do before the gun hits your shoulder. In the field you will pass through the ready position for a split second before reaching the final lined-up position. When game is flushed in your easy swing area, your body should immediately begin to swing with the bird's flight. At the same time and as part of the swing, shift your weight to the left foot, tilt your head forward, raise your left

hand to eye level and place the gun in that hand. You are now in the ready position and from here you can raise the gun to your shoulder in an instant.

It is very important that you start to swing as soon as you see the bird. If your head, shoulders and arms have been positioned during the swing, as a part of it, raising the gun becomes incidental; when it is mounted, you will find it pointed at the target. Since your body has been pre-aimed while swinging, there is no other place for the gun to point.

If game gets up outside your easy swing area, you will need to change your stance. This is done by taking a *small* step with the left foot, to one side or the other, pivoting on the right one. As you take this step, your weight shifts automatically to the left leg. The step becomes a part of your swing and, at the same time, your head, shoulders and arms start moving into position.

During the swing your body works as a whole. Various parts must move to assume different positions, but these moves must blend into one to give you the smooth swing you need. Your swing must be rhythmical, and acquiring this rhythm will take practice.

Rhythm in body movement is often called "muscular coordination," and coordination in this sense requires arrangement of the component moves in correct order or sequence. The parts of the body which must be coordinated in swinging a gun are the feet, hips, shoulders and arms, and the hands which hold the gun. They must be moved in this sequence for the swing to be rhythmical; from the inside out if you will think of your arms as the spokes of a wheel, with energy flowing from hub to rim. Early in these moves your weight shifts to the left leg and your head tilts forward. Your last act is to mount the gun. Don't rush it. There is more time than you think—for if the butt is brought up earlier you will be locked in at that point, unable properly to position your body and complete the swing.

In order to make these actions more automatic, practice them at home. Practice gun mounting and swinging on a target in slow motion first, to be sure you have the right sequence of moves, using an imaginary line on the wall as the flight of a bird. With a little practice you will begin to feel each movement blending smoothly into the next, which is so essential to the overall rhythm.

When hunting, try not to become so absorbed in mounting the gun that you neglect your feet. Although proper raising of gun to shoulder is very important, this act should not preclude attention to the rest of your

Changing stance to the left. When birds get up to the left, take a step to the left with your left foot before mounting the gun. Note that the head is tilted forward, the weight shifted and the left hand raised to eye level as the turn is being made, so that the gun can be mounted instantly when it is completed.

69

body. *The position of your feet determines your easy‑ swing area*, as discussed in the last chapter, *and often a step with the left foot starts the swing of your body.* If the feet get mixed up with each other, as may happen in a duck blind, or if one of them is out of position on a steep hillside, it is very difficult to bring the gun up on target. Under these conditions most shots will be missed because your stance was wrong to begin with. So think of your feet when hunting, judge the ground ahead of you, and walk slowly. Should game get up suddenly, you will have a better chance of stopping on the proper foot.

GUN HANDLING IN THE FIELD

Safety is just as critical a subject in the field as it is anywhere else. There are several safe ways to carry a gun when hunting, but the best of all is *with the muzzle pointed up.* You can hold it in either the right or left hand, alternating so that neither becomes tired, but there is one rule always to remember: The carrying hand should hold the gun at the place where it must be when the gun is fired, or be able to move into the firing position without delay.

The simplest way to carry a gun is to rest it on your shoulder with the right hand holding it at the grip. The trigger guard should be facing up and the muzzle pointed up. The exact position of the hand is determined by the length of the trigger finger, as described earlier. Place that finger on the trigger guard and you now have one hand in the shooting position. When you wish to shoot, shift your weight to the left foot, raise your left hand to eye level with palm up, tilt your head forward,

70

*How to carry a gun in the field. In both cases the guns are angled
so that the muzzles point up. Note that in the position on the left
the trigger finger is safely on the trigger guard.*

When sitting in a duck blind, orient your feet and bring the left hand to eye level before getting to your feet. In other words, put your upper body in the ready position and get the gun moving before you get up.

and flip the fore-end of the gun into the palm of your left hand. In a split second, you are in the ready position.

In a duck blind, you can lean the gun against the wall or hold it on your lap. The latter is the safer position. If the gun is leaning against the wall, reach for it with your left hand, holding it at the fore-end. Then lift and turn it at the same time so you can place your right hand on the grip. Do not stand up until your left hand reaches eye level. In other words, *the gun first, then you.* If the gun is resting on your lap, both hands should be in their shooting positions, but here, again, the gun goes up first and you follow.

Carrying a gun in both hands can be very tiring. Nevertheless, they should each be in position when you think you may have an immediate shot, such as when your dog is on point and a bird is about to be flushed.

The best position when standing, waiting for game. The gun is braced on the belt. From here you can move quickly into shooting position just by lifting your left hand to eye level and shifting your weight to the left foot.

When standing still, waiting for a flight, an easy position is to hold the gun in your right hand, at the grip, with the butt resting on your hip. From here you can easily move into either the ready or the lined-up position.

There is an axiom in the gun business that accidents only happen with unloaded guns. But there is little consolation to the dead victim of gun carelessness that he was shot with an "unloaded" gun. Indeed, a gun is unloaded only when you can see its empty chambers.

73

The authors talking things over during a Mexican quail hunt. Note the safe position of each gun—I've got my pump gun pointed skyward and its action open, while Beck's over-and-under is broken and would be safe even if it were loaded.

It is only common courtesy to your hunting partners to carry a double-barrel gun with the action broken, or an automatic or pump gun with breech open, when you are not actually hunting. This is the only safe way for all persons involved. There is absolutely no excuse for carelessness in handling a gun. Such lack of consideration for others is criminal.

Permitting the muzzle end of your gun to dip into mud, snow or water can result in a blown barrel, which is another good reason for carrying a gun with the muzzle pointed up. It does not take a solidly plugged barrel to bulge or blow out when the gun is fired; even a small piece of leaf, twig or shell wad can cause serious damage.

Always load and unload while standing still. There is no advantage in trying to load while on the run for you really save no time. You can load much faster and certainly more safely if you give it your undivided attention. Also, should you flush game while loading on the run, you will not be ready to shoot. Load from your right-hand pocket, since this is quicker. The weight of the shells holds your hunting jacket in position so it will not wrinkle or slide up on your shoulder. As the weight goes down on the right, transfer shells from the left-hand pocket.

74

Resting your gun muzzle on the ground is a fine way to ruin a beautiful gun. It doesn't take much debris to cause a bulge, or worse—even a twig or a bit of snow can do it.

An unfortunate mistake sometimes made is to load a 20-gauge shell in a 12-gauge gun or a 28-gauge shell in a 20-gauge gun. This can result in a badly bulged or blown-out barrel. The smaller shell will slide down just far enough in the barrel to allow the larger one to be loaded on top of it. There is no need to explain what takes place when the trigger is pulled, and you're lucky if only a badly damaged gun results. If any two persons in your shooting family use different gauge guns, make absolutely certain that the shells do not get mixed up. I find it helpful to separate gauges by color, since most manufacturers nowadays use different colors for the various gauges.

CHAPTER **6**

Hints on Hunting

Successful hunting of any game, winged or four-footed, depends as much on a knowledge of its habits as on shooting skill. Novice hunters can spend some very rewarding time watching the movements of game, and even old-timers, when new in a particular area, should check it out before the hunt, unless, of course, they are with a guide or companion who knows the country.

Game will act differently in different places at different times of the day, but usually it moves on a strict time schedule except when interfered with by a change in weather conditions, such as rain or a sudden shift in temperature. Feeding is generally done in the early morning and late afternoon, while the rest of the day is spent in sleeping or staying under cover. Thus the best times to observe movement are after sunup and possibly late in the afternoon, when cover is left for feeding or drinking grounds.

Knowing when and where movement will occur and for what purpose can assure good shooting. Doves, for example, will commute between their roosting trees and water and feeding grounds. Knowing the times for these moves and the flight pattern to be followed has obvious advantages. When walking up for pheasant, quail or the like, remember that birds have very keen vision and hearing but that they have difficulty looking into the sun, and that any wind carries sound with it. So start your hunt into the wind and with the sun behind you, where possible.

A working knowledge of the hunting area is also helpful. You will be less likely to lose your way and you will know of other places to hunt should your first choice not work out.

Watch all birds at which you have shot and mark well where they fall. Never take your eye off that spot or you will lose it, but if you don't find the bird when you reach it, put something down as a marker — your hat or a handkerchief — and start walking round that in ever widening circles. If birds do not fall immediately, their flight may tell you that they will. A slight change in direction can mean a hit and that the bird will soon land or die. Birds that fly off with both legs down can usually be found where they land, but approach them cautiously and with a loaded gun for some are able to take flight again without a starting run. A bird "towering," or steeply climbing, after being shot at, is apt to fall stone dead. A bird flying in a circle has probably been hit in one eye and, after landing, can easily lose itself. Birds dropping with one wing up are usually runners, especially if the head is up.

A wounded bird, particularly a runner, should not be approached directly in open country. Take a course forty to fifty yards to right or left, just about out of shot range, go past the bird and circle around it, gradually tightening the ring; and when finally within range, approach with the sun behind you. The bird will feel secure after you first pass it by at a safe distance and is then more apt to stay put as you tighten the circle.

Always kill wounded birds immediately by wringing their necks until you feel the head disconnected from the vertebrae. They should be quickly put out of their misery and never put in your hunting jacket "half dead."

In a blind, remain still. Movement attracts attention more than anything else. Do not squirm around or move your gun barrel and, if possible, don't move your head. Glasses and even your eyes will give you away, as will your lighter colored face, so cover them with a wide-brimmed hat.

When a covey of quail gets up or a flight of ducks comes over, remember always to single out one bird to shoot. If you fire indiscriminately into the mass you will hit nothing. With quail, take one of the first to get up and then look for another, but remember that you can't make a double unless you hit the first. On crossing and incoming birds it sometimes pays to take a rear one first as those in front will probably still be in range and not be disturbed by the shot behind them.

Watching a good bird dog work is half the fun of hunting. In addition, you'll get better shots and lose fewer cripples.

When hunting with a dog, start early and give him a good run before you begin to work him. This lets him blow off steam and settle down to the serious business at hand. Never over-guide your dog with too frequent commands. If he has not received sufficient training before you hunt him, he will not learn out there when both of you are keyed up. Don't constantly whistle and yell at him, for he probably won't listen anyway and you will only become more frustrated. Finally, never underestimate the ability of a dog. Believe him when he goes on point and check it out. The chances are that his is a better nose than yours. I will always remember Frank, an English pointer with a radar nose. One time he went on point and we shot the pheasant, but he stayed on point, just turning his head a bit to the left. My companion thought he was still pointing where the flushed bird had been, but knowing Frank as I did, I realized that there must be another bird. We checked it out and, sure enough, there was.

A dog should always be under control and hunt for you, not himself, but sometimes it is best to let him have his own way. This is especially true when tracking a wounded bird; let a good dog work it out by himself. I have often seen dogs take off in the "wrong" direction only to come up with a retrieve. A good dog can and does distinguish between the smells of different birds and will follow unerringly the tracks of the right one. ·

Walk slowly when hunting, with or without a dog. A slow-walking hunter is a more sure-footed one, better able to position his feet properly for a quick shot, nor will he tire as fast during a long day's hunt. A steady, unhurried pace will take you a surprisingly long way. And it gives a dog a chance to work the ground properly and without feeling pushed.

A good hunter makes each shot count and does not blaze away at just anything in sight. I learned this fact early in life from Old Rip, one of the greatest dogs I have ever been privileged to hunt over. He belonged to my father's friend, Field Marshal Kontz, whose son Sándor and I hunted together in our childhood. When we were termed "safe," we were allowed to take the Marshal's German shorthair and to share a 20-gauge gun between us, shooting alternately. Rip would point and work for us, like the old pro he was, until we missed three birds in a row. After that he turned for home and no amount of whistling, calling or coaxing could bring him back that day. The hunt was over and we soon learned to take no haphazard shots.

If you stop in cover for any reason, be on the alert for a few seconds. This is often a time when birds will flush if they are around. As long as they can hear you

Mexican quail shooting: Beck on the left, in a good ready position, myself shooting, and our guide Leo Peterson a couple of steps to the rear. Hunters should stay approximately in line when walking up game.

walking, they feel more or less secure, but when you stop they think you have spotted them, and so try to get away. Therefore, when you only fire one shot, don't hurry to reload. Wait a few seconds to be sure another bird doesn't get up while your gun is open for reloading.

CHOICE OF LOAD AND CHOKE

Though your own shooting skill and knowledge of the game you are hunting will always be the major determinants of the size of your bag, there is a third factor which will exert a very considerable influence on your hunting success — the appropriateness of the loads and choke you are using to the game being hunted.

81

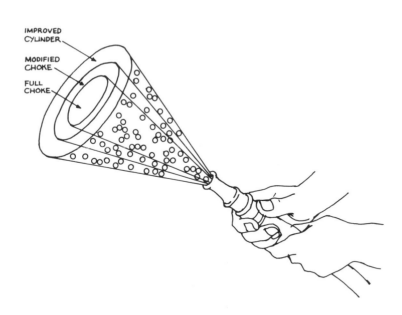

IMPROVED CYLINDER

MODIFIED CHOKE

FULL CHOKE

Choke regulates the circumference of the shot pattern much as an adjustable nozzle controls the spray of water from a garden hose.

The importance of pattern density has already been mentioned, along with the example that a shotgun shoots a spray of pellets much as a garden hose sprays water. A look at the illustration will show you why the pattern will be denser at the narrow end of the cone than at the large end. Thus, as the distance from shooter to target is increased, the density fades out until the target can easily slip through the pattern without being hit.

The range of your gun can, however, be lengthened by increasing the density of the pattern, and this can be done in two ways. First, by tightening the spray of pellets through constricting or "choking" the muzzle; and second, by putting more pellets in the pattern through the use of high-brass or magnum shells.

Let's discuss these subjects in order, starting with the choice of choke. The range of different chokes is classified according to the percentage of a shell's pellets which fall within a 30-inch circle at a distance of 40 yards.

The four principal choke designations are:

Skeet choke, used mostly for skeet shooting; 40 – 50 percent pattern.

Improved-Cylinder choke, designed for close shooting of game; 50 percent pattern.

Modified choke, perhaps the most versatile; 60 percent pattern.

Full choke, the best for long ranges; a pattern of 70 percent or better.

The pattern percentages given are approximations only and variations of plus or minus 5 percent can be expected depending on the gun and shells used. There are also other designations for intermediate degrees of choke, such as Quarter choke (55 percent) and Improved-Modified (65 percent), but the basic ones are those listed above.

Of course, the more open chokes permit the shot pattern to open up more rapidly, thus giving a wider pattern sooner. Skeet or open Improved-Cylinder patterns are unquestionably the best for shooting at short ranges, such as you will find in skeet (where the maximum range is about 25 yards) or in brush hunting for woodcock, partridges, quail and the like.

The Modified choke falls between the open bores and the Full choke, and is considered the best for all-around shooting. It is especially good in shooting pheasants over dogs, ducks over decoys, and in dove hunting. It also makes an excellent first barrel for a double-barrel gun. The Full choke is the tightest of all and is the long-range barrel, most suitable for pass shooting at duck and geese and late-season pheasant. The maximum range of a shotgun shooting a low-base shell in a full-choke barrel is about 40 yards. The Improved-Cylinder choke gives an effective range of 30 yards and the modified choke, 35 yards.

These ranges can be extended by from 5 to 7 yards for each one-quarter ounce of additional shot used in a high-base or magnum shell. However, before concluding that only magnum shells should be used for long-range work, you should consider the fact that these loads have no more velocity than regular high-base loads, and sometimes less. So while they produce a denser pattern, they may require longer leads. Remember, too, that it makes no sense to use magnum loads with small shot. (Shot comes in various sizes from No. 2 to No. 9, the larger the number the smaller the size.) The velocity of small shot drops off so quickly that the benefit of the denser pattern is lost at long ranges because of the absence of needed penetration.

Shooters who claim to have killed birds at 65 yards or more have usually either misjuged the distance, or have had one or two lucky pellets hit the bird's brain, spine or some other vital spot. It is practically impossible to hit with any consistency at this range, even if you should have the "miracle shell." There are very few shooters capable of judging the correct leads at such distances.

In other words, the fact that a shell has a lot of kick

does not necessarily insure good results. Loads must be balanced and should be tested for pattern and penetration to suit the gun in which they will be used. This holds for both factory-loaded ammunition and reloads. Shotguns are erratic performers, and as of this writing, no one knows exactly why some guns shoot well with one shell and not with another. We do know of several ways to regulate patterns by altering the choke or some other barrel specification, but even if you fire ten identical guns with the same choke designation, the chances are that each will shoot a somewhat different pattern. There are always some loads and shot sizes that a particular gun will "like" and shoot well, and in most cases this will not be a "hot" load. Light, well-balanced loads usually give the best results. And sometimes just changing shot size, from 8 to 7½ or from 6 to 5, will improve performance.

PATTERNING

In order to find out what kind of choke your gun has in actual practice, and to learn which shells it performs best with, you must shoot some patterns with it. Patterning a shotgun is relatively easy. All you need is a supply of large size paper sheets, about four feet square, and a still day. Tack up a sheet forty yards away and place a marker at which to aim in the center. Be sure to shoot "off-hand" at the target, without any rest. A rested barrel, or even one held short, can give an entirely erroneous pattern, especially with double-barrel guns, so hold the gun as you would when shooting in the field. Aim at the center marker, but do not worry about hitting the paper squarely in the center. Select the center of your pattern and draw a thirty-inch circle around it. Then count the number of pellet holes within the circle, calculate the percentage of shot that hit within it and compare with other loads fired.

Just as important as the right pattern percentage is an even distribution of the shot, with as few "holes" as possible inside the circle. A pronounced concentration of shot in the center is not a useful pattern, nor is a blotchy one; the latter often indicates too much push behind the shot. There are more complicated ways of evaluating patterns but the test described above is adequate for the average shooter. He must, however, take the trouble to shoot not less than five patterns with each load from each barrel to be used, and to mark each sheet with the relevant data.

Penetration is another factor to be tested. A few old phone books or stacks of magazines are all that is needed. Shoot at them from forty yards and count the number of pages penetrated; the differences will be quite apparent. Incidentally, while testing for pattern coverage and penetration, it's not a bad idea to also test for point of impact. This will show just where your gun shoots and, while guns made by reliable makers shoot where they should, I have seen new factory guns that were off as much as two feet at forty yards. Also, barrels may have become bent slightly due to improper handling and this will show up in the testing, though it might not be apparent to the average shooter.

To pattern a gun for point of impact, stand about fifteen yards from the target and shoot off-hand, carefully aiming at the bull's-eye. At this short distance the shot pellets will be sufficiently concentrated to give you a good idea of where the gun hits. Shoot five patterns with each barrel and if either of them shoots off, you had better have the gun examined by a competent gunsmith.

Before proceeding to specific suggestions on the various loads to be used in hunting different kinds of game, I would like to consider some of the basic principles involved.

If you use a shell with large size shot, you will, of course, have a less dense pattern than if you use a shell with smaller shot because there will be many more pellets of the smaller size to cover a given area. This brings up the first important factor concerning effective shotgun shooting: You must have a pattern dense enough to assure that an adequate amount of shot reaches the target. Indeed, you can blast away all day long without touching a target if the pattern of pellets is so thin that it can slip through unscathed.

The second factor is penetration. No matter how dense a pattern is, unless the pellets have the velocity needed to penetrate to a vital organ or to break bones, your shooting is ineffective and you only cripple birds, leaving them to die after days or weeks of agony.

Therefore, always remember that you must have both (1) adequate density and (2) adequate penetration.

For small birds like quail or dove, you obviously need a denser pattern than you do for geese. And you should use a pellet size between the two for pheasants and ducks. Also bear in mind that small shot loses its velocity much faster than large shot, regardless of how fast it is discharged from the gun. For example, a handful of sand thrown as hard as you can will fall to the ground quickly, while a handful of gravel, thrown with the same force, will continue much farther. The rule, therefore, is to *choose the largest size pellet possible that will make a dense enough pattern for the game you wish to shoot.*

The reason for this in addition to the ballistic reason, is that shot size also affects your enjoyment of a bird at home. My friend Frank Adams does a lot of hunting and is quite particular about the size shot used on game. He says there is a big difference between eating a pheasant or a duck that has been killed with No. 5 or No. 4 shot, compared to No. 7½. So much of a contrast that if he is shooting these birds with someone using No. 7½, he makes very sure at the end of the hunt to take only the birds he shot. He does not like to eat a bird that is filled with a lot of small pellets. The smaller the size shot used to kill, the more pellets there will be to chew on.

RECOMMENDED LOADS

SMALL BIRDS

Railbird,	Low-Base Shell No. 8 shot, to
Snipe, etc.	High-Base Shell No. 7½ shot
Dove, Quail,	Low-Base Shell No. 7½ shot, to
Hungarian	High-Base Shell No. 7½ shot
Partridge, etc.	

LARGER BIRDS AND RABBITS

Grouse,	High-Base Shell No. 6 shot, to
Sand Grouse,	High-Base Shell No. 5 shot
Pheasant,	
Cottontail	
Rabbit, etc.	
Ducks	High-Base Shell No. 5 to No. 4 shot; when using magnum loads, No. 4 or No. 2 shot

LARGE BIRDS

Geese	High-Base Shell No. 4 or No. 2 shot; when using magnum shells, No. 2 shot

Small shot sizes in magnum loads are practically useless, and do nothing that the larger shot sizes don't do better.

CHAPTER **7**

Practice Devices and Shooting Games

Practice is just as essential to good shooting as it is to the fine performance of any other demanding activity. It is not surprising then that through the years many ingenious devices have been developed for that purpose. They range from the relatively simple compressed air streams shot at targets, and miniature targets shot with .22 shot shells, to more sophisticated electronic gadgets. Many were designed for indoor use and thus employ substitutes for regular ammunition. One is a small flashlight to be mounted on a gun with the switch connected to the trigger. When the trigger is pulled a spot of light appears on the wall. This is called the Shotlight, and occasionally I still use one for training.

During my last visit to London, Mr. Harry Lawrence, then managing director of Purdey's, showed me his latest invention. A small box with a photoelectric eye runs back and forth on the ceiling of their famous "long room." An electric cartridge is loaded in the gun and when the box is "hit," it lights up; otherwise, a speck of light shows on the wall. This is very helpful to them in gun fitting. They can see how a customer mounts the gun on a moving target and make adjustments in the stock as they may be needed.

I was introduced to shooting games at an early age. One Sunday my parents took me to a pigeon shoot at which some ancient glass balls were also being shot. These were a little smaller than a tennis ball and were filled with feathers. A simple flat spring device threw them almost straight up in the air about 60 feet. When hit, the feathers really flew. Right then I decided to become a glass ball shooting champion, and I went home and immediately built a glass ball thrower. It consisted of a flat piece of wood placed in the fork of a branch hammered into the ground. When a fallen apple was placed on one end of the flat piece, and the other end was hit hard, the apple flew into the air. This contraption worked well until I ran out of shells. To my dismay, my parents did not share my hopes for a brilliant future at this game and since they were reluctant to purchase shells for rotten apple shooting, my little show came to an end.

Anyway, interest in glass ball shooting had long since been dealt a fatal blow. When Carver and other crack shots from America came to Europe and began shattering them with a .22 rifle shotgunners turned to clay target shooting. Why they are called "clay," I do not know, for they are actually made out of pitch and limestone. The clay birds were used originally for practice in the field, but this shooting soon became a competitive sport — first as trap and later as skeet shooting.

I am often asked whether trap or skeet shooting helps your hunting, and my answer is always an unqualified "yes." The more you handle your gun, whether you practice mounting it in the living room or shoot at clay targets outdoors, the better you will come to know it. And the better acquainted you are with your gun, the more you accustom yourself to noise and recoil, to gun mounting and trigger pull, to loading and unloading and to the many small acts that are so much a part of shooting, the better you will shoot. Your mind and muscles will be conditioned to the point where many moves will be made almost without thinking. Hitting the clay birds may even become mechanical, but the shooting will keep you tuned up for the field.

There are two kinds of trap shooting, American and International. In American trap, the target is thrown by an oscillating target thrower which alters the direction of each throw. This machine is 16 yards from the shooters and is located in a trap house. The rules require that targets be thrown approximately 50 yards and within an approximate 94-degree angle.

Twenty-five targets constitute a round of trap shooting. There are five shooting stations back of the trap house, numbered 1 to 5 from left to right. Each shooter fires five times from each station and the squad rotates

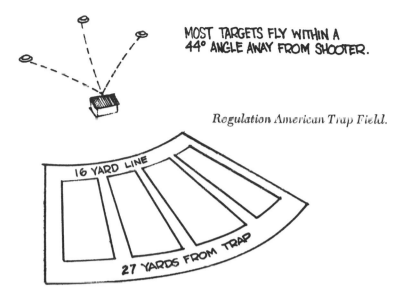

MOST TARGETS FLY WITHIN A
44° ANGLE AWAY FROM SHOOTER.

Regulation American Trap Field.

after each string by shifting to the right, the man at
No. 5 moving to No. 1 station. All shooting is done from
the 16-yard stations except in handicap trap, when a
shooter may be required to move as far back as 27
yards, depending on his handicap. When shooting doubles, two targets are thrown at the same time, instead
of one.

The International game differs from American trap
in several ways. The trap house on an International field
contains fifteen separate traps arranged in a straight
trench in groups of three. Sixteen and a half yards to
the rear is a line of five shooting stations, one station for
each group of three traps. The traps throw their targets
within a 45-degree angle right or left of the center trap
in each group. Each trap is set at a fixed angle for one
day of shooting, but the shooter never knows which of
the three traps in his group will throw the next target.
This is determined by a lottery machine which selects

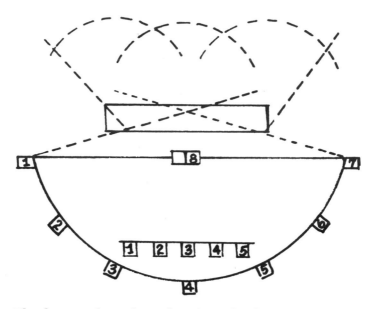

The diagram above shows the relationship between the 15-trap International Trap layout and a standard American skeet field.

the same hundred targets for each shooter, but in different sequence.

Shooters move from one station to the next after each target, but two shots may be fired at a target without penalty. There are six shooters in a squad, the sixth man standing behind the No. 1 shooter. After the latter has fired, he steps to the right to take his place on the second station while the sixth man moves onto Station No. 1.

In International trap, the targets are thrown about 80 yards and their initial velocity is nearly three times that of the American type. The greater speed of the International targets makes them more difficult to hit, and using both barrels on a single target teaches the shooter how to correct with his second shot.

94

The other popular shooting game is skeet, and here, also, there are International and American rules. Skeet was developed to give the hunter shots more nearly simulating the angles encountered in upland shooting. A single trap was used originally and the shooters moved around it in a full circle. Later, in order to minimize the amount of land required, two traps were installed opposite each other to retain all the angles.

The principal difference between trap and skeet shooting is that in trap the targets are always going away from you, while in skeet you have a variety of angling shots as well as going away and incoming birds. But while the trap constantly varies the outgoing angles of trap targets, skeet targets always fly the same path and the shooters move from station to station to change the angle of their shots.

A skeet field is laid out with two trap houses, a high house on the left and a low house to the right, and eight shooting stations. (See diagram.) The targets are thrown over the center post near Station 8 at a height of approximately 15 feet and they travel about 60 yards. A round consists of 25 targets, and at each station the shooter fires first at one thrown from the high house and then one from the low house. Doubles are shot on Stations 1, 2, 6 and 7. If he hits all targets, the shooter will have an extra shell and this is usually shot from Station 7. The extra shell is also used as a repeat after the first miss.

In American skeet the shooter may call for the target with the gun at his shoulder in the shooting position, but the International rules require the butt of the gun to be touching his hip. Also, under International rules, the target's appearance may be delayed for as much as three seconds after calling for it. Thus, with skeet as well as trap, the International system requires greater ability and will give the shooter better practice for hunting.

There is another game that uses clay birds which probably requires more skill than either skeet or trap. This is the quail walk, and it offers you better practice for the field because it is closer to the real thing. Unfortunately, there are not many in America (they are not well known), but they are quite popular abroad, especially in England. Shooting a round must be done by one person at a time, not in squads, so the sport does not lend itself readily to competition because of the time involved.

Quail walks should be set up where it is easy to simulate hunting conditions, in country with bushes

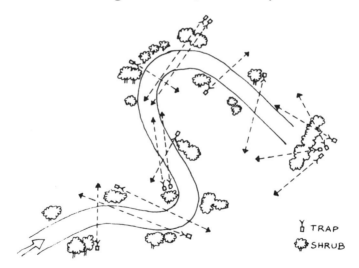

A Typical Quail Walk. At least 15 traps should be used.

and a few trees around to complete the picture (see drawing). At least fifteen practice-type traps are strategically located behind bushes where they cannot be seen when walking the course. A typical walk is shown in the accompanying drawing but many variations are possible. All traps are hand sprung by someone walking behind the shooter, or by an electric eye. I have always found these quail walks most interesting to shoot, and when there are enough traps not to require tripping the same ones every time, the targets are hard to memorize and present a new challenge with each walk.

Probably the most difficult shooting game of all is flyer or live pigeon shooting. You find little of this in America — it has long since been outlawed in most states, and probably rightly so — but Europeans regard it as the sport requiring the greatest skill. Large flyer shoots are still held in France, Italy, Spain and other

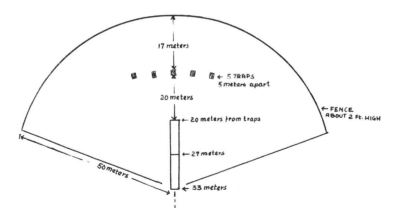

Dimensions of a European Live-Bird Field.

The live-bird field at Valencia, Spain, site of the 1968 World Championship. All five traps are visible, and a bird has just been sprung from No. 4. The white-shirted trap boys at right retrieve the shot birds and reload the traps.

European countries for big money prizes. As the name implies, live pigeons, specially bred for the purpose, are used as targets. One bird is placed in each of five collapsible boxes, or traps as they are called, set in a line at right angles to the shooting station. The shooter stands from 20 to 33 meters back, depending on his handicap, but championship matches are shot at 27 meters. The field is surrounded by a fence about two feet high which, at its closest point, is approximately 17 meters from the traps. All birds must be dropped and picked up inside the fence either by a dog or a trap boy.

Two shots are allowed. The bird must be in the air for the first shot, but it can be, and often is, killed on the ground with the second. On serious shoots, *Zurito* pigeons are used. These are a special breed of rock pigeon — small, gray and very fast. When the trap opens, these birds take off like lightning, and in a stiff wind they present a real test of shooting ability.

98

Two outstanding live-bird shooters: Above is George Neary, one of few Americans to have excelled at this sport, and below is Alexander de Dora, three-time winner of the coveted Grand Prix de Monte Carlo. Neary adopts a rather high right elbow, a variation favored by many trap shooters, and de Dora prefers a rather "long" left arm. These are personal idiosyncrasies, but all shooters should emulate the general ease and solidity of their positions.

Prizes for flyer shoots are usually in cash and sometimes the stakes are high. To eliminate any possibility of cheating, electrical devices are used both to open the traps by voice and to select at random the particular trap for each shot. Birds killed are usually donated to the kitchens of hospitals or other charitable organizations. Guns for flyer shooting are mostly 12-gauge double-barrel, side-by-sides or over-and-unders, of medium weight and choked either full and full or modified and full.

While there is practically no flyer shooting in America, and quail walks are hard to find, there are plenty of trap and skeet fields on which to practice. All it takes is a little will power to make the effort, but once made, you will find it most rewarding.

CHAPTER **8**

Hunting Abroad

Hunting small game in Europe has become increasingly available and popular since World War II. Many hunting grounds that used to be accessible only to a select number of invited guests may now be leased by those who can afford it, and enterprising travel agents now book shooting trips abroad at prices which prove within reach of many bird hunting devotees.

The rough or walk-up shooting for European partridge, pheasant, woodcock and quail is not much different from that found in this country except that the going is usually easier. You walk mostly in cultivated fields, stubble or meticulously cleared woods. This kind of hunting generally offers no great novelty to an American, but it does afford a chance to learn something of European ways.

The true European sport is driven-bird shooting, for Scottish grouse, Spanish partridge and pheasants wherever found. On most pheasant drives you also get a variety of other small game such as rabbits and hares. The sellers of these shoots will sometimes guarantee as many as a thousand birds bagged in a day by parties of ten to fourteen shooters. This number takes on added significance when you consider that even a very good shot who has little or no experience in driven-bird shooting, will do well to hit 50 percent of the birds at which he shoots. In fact, a ratio of three shells per bird is considered a good average. Shooting on driven grouse or partridge is some of the most difficult to be had anywhere.

Most European game will be found on private hunting preserves. Its raising and protection is in the hands of highly skilled gamekeepers and their staffs, and these experts have preserved the game year after year at pretty much the same level. It is usually some climatic or other natural disaster which depletes their numbers, not the shooting. If the hatch is poor in any year, the shooting season may be closed until the stock has been replenished. When shooting pheasants, it is usual to shoot only the cock birds. In most European countries a shooter cannot obtain a hunting license until he has passed an examination to show not only his ability to handle a gun safely but also his knowledge of game. These are some of the measures which have been used to conserve the game for future generations.

Unfortunately, in spite of all this care, the partridge population in parts of Europe is now perilously low. This sad condition is due primarily to the use of pesticides and other chemicals rather than to excessive shooting pressure. Only last year I hunted in Austria at a place that used to yield two hundred partridges per gun, walked up between 10 A.M. and 3 P.M. This time we had great difficulty in bagging twenty-five.

Hunting in the pre-war days was quite an experience. A classic type, which is seldom seen today, is called "strip" hunting, or by its German name, *Streifen Jagd*. On these shoots a large rectangular piece of land, several miles long and a mile or so wide, was selected. The shooters were stationed on one of the narrow ends, 150 to 200 yards apart, while the beaters took positions on the sides about fifty yards from each other. The entire group formed a "U" and moved toward the open end. On reaching a certain point, the beaters turned in and closed the opening. The hunters then stopped and the beaters began the drive back, pushing the enclosed game toward the shooters. On the drive down, very little game had escaped. The flanks were about a mile long and were able to hold nearly all game within the "U."

The most famous of these shoots were those conducted by Count Louis Karolyi. In his book *Weidwerk Ohne Gleichen* he states that between 1930 and 1937 over 226,000 hares, pheasants and partridges were bagged at Totmegyer, Hungary, the best year (1933) accounting for 37,616 pieces. His estates were probably the most famous in Europe for small game shooting, and some of his guests managed to shoot over 800 pieces in a single day.

These shoots were managed with all the precision of a military maneuver. Four hundred beaters were hired, and each shooter had his own staff consisting of a loader, an assistant loader, a shell and coat carrier, two pairs of game carriers with long poles on which to hang the game, a boy to pick up and tie the legs of game together and two pheasant and partridge carriers — in all, about ten people. Behind this group, about 400 yards to the rear, came a cart drawn by four oxen, into which the game was loaded. During a day's shoot, which covered two strips, the bag would run from two to five thousand pieces, usually distributed evenly between hares, pheasants and partridges. An individual hunter would bag from two to six hundred pieces.

The over-all assemblage on one of these shoots, in addition to the hunters and their own staffs, included: twenty oxcarts for game, drawn by four oxen each; three light carriages to transport shooters, and the same for loaders; one carriage for shells; five for the gamekeepers; one horn blower to give signals; and six horsemen to keep the lines straight.

Driven bird shoots are just what the name implies. The birds are driven to or over the shooters who are waiting for them in blinds, or "butts" as they are called. The butts are built to blend into the surrounding landscape and are placed in strategic positions behind knolls or ridges so the birds will have difficulty in spotting them. They are spread 50-100 yards apart and are mostly in a straight line. The shooters and their loaders stand in the butts facing toward the beaters, and the latter start the drive from a mile or two away, pushing the game toward the shooters.

On large drives each shooter uses two guns. These should be of the same gauge, perfectly matched, and have automatic safeties which go on when the gun is opened for loading. The guns should be on the light side and with fairly open bores, usually improved cylinder and modified chokes. I am speaking, of course, of double-barrel guns, side-by-sides being preferred since they are easier to load quickly than the over-and-unders. Automatics and pumps are usually frowned upon for these shoots, but if they are used you will need three guns and two loaders because though they need not be plugged, as in this country, they take longer to load than they do to shoot.

While the shooter's marksmanship is of paramount importance, a good loader is very essential if many birds are to be bagged. The loader stands at the shooter's right and a step behind him with the second gun, loaded and held at the grip in his right hand. After the first gun is fired, the shooter lifts his right forearm from the elbow, bringing the gun to the perpendicular. His left hand stays in the shooting position with the palm open and up. The loader then places the loaded gun in the open palm, holding that gun at the grip with his right hand, and, at the same time, he takes the empty gun with his left hand, grasping it at the forearm. A slight turn to the right by the shooter will often speed up the exchange. If the shooter has turned for an extreme left bird, a good loader will step forward, or back for a turn to the right. Guns should be exchanged even though only one barrel has been fired. The shooter should concentrate solely on the game and never concern himself with loading. Fast teamwork between shooter and loader can be spectacular, and in the "good old days," when

Bird-shooting heaven—a Scottish grouse moor. My loader, George, is standing to my right in the butt. Taking birds with both barrels of a pair of guns on a single drive takes skillful gun handling as well as brilliant shooting. However, kills with a fifth barrel are not unknown!

we took our own loaders to a shoot, we always had a loaded gun in hand when needed. Unfortunately, in recent years on paid shoots, I have found no top-flight loaders.

The procedure just described is the English way of exchanging guns. In Spain the loader is called a *secretario* and he sits in front of the shooter, facing him. The empty gun must be handed down and the loaded one picked up. This is a more time-consuming operation than the English one and is less efficient.

A few pointers for those who are not familiar with shooting conditions in Europe. Take along your local hunting license as this may serve as the basis for obtaining one in Europe. Do not argue with your host or whoever directs the shoot even though you think you know better. He probably knows something of which you are not aware and in the long run you will be better off to have said nothing. Don't boast of what you have shot, or the quantity; your shooting will be sufficiently eloquent. And don't drink liquor while shooting. I had a bad time a year or two back living down the performance of another American party that had preceded me in Scotland. They had brought bottles into the butts and shot so dangerously that the beaters threatened to quit.

Always follow the basic safety rules. When not shooting open and unload your gun and carry it that way. When swinging on a bird flying over the line of the butts to your right or left, don't let your gun pass through the line of shooters. Take it off your shoulder and don't bring it up again until you have passed the line. Don't try to shoot away your neighbor's birds by shooting in front of him, and don't shoot at incomers after the beaters are in range. Always know where people who are participating in the shoot are located.

In some places it is customary to shoot wounded running birds on the ground. If you are asked to do this, be careful of ricochets; they are always dangerous.

Clothing for European shooting should be on the dark side, and for driven game it should be warm since many of these shoots are held in the fall. Leave your red or yellow hat at home and take no bandanas or loud colors with you, but a sweater, scarf and lightweight rain gear can be most useful.

PART TWO

Selection and Care of Guns and Accessories

CHAPTER **9**

Types of Guns
and How To
Choose One

Many years ago when I was starting as a gun salesman, I showed a pair of fine English guns to a customer who wished to use them abroad. When I named the price, he asked why these guns were so much more expensive than the others he'd looked at. "It's like the difference between a Rolls Royce and a Ford," I assured him. "Both cars will get you there, but what a difference in finish and handling!" My customer said he didn't agree with the analogy, so I didn't press the point. But when the sale was concluded and he gave the shipping instructions, you can imagine how I felt when he said that his name was Henry Ford, II.

111

Needless to say, I've been kidded about this episode for many years.

I mention it here to illustrate that serviceable shotguns can be found within a very wide price range, from well under a hundred dollars to several thousand. However, the size of the purchaser's pocketbook is only one of the factors involved in choosing a gun; the physical make-up of the hunter who will use it and the particular use to be made of it must also be reckoned with. Perhaps the first considerations should be the choice of gauge and type of action. The most popular gauges for hunting are 12, 16, 20; the smaller the number the bigger the gauge. (The old gunsmiths determined gauges by the number of spherical lead balls of identical size it took to weigh a pound. The only exception to this is the so-called 410 gauge, which is really a bore size measured in thousandths of an inch and more properly termed a .410 bore.)

The basic types of shotgun actions are:
1. double-barrel, over-and-under;
2. double-barrel, side-by-side;
3. semiautomatic or autoloader, herein called automatic;
4. slide or pump-action;
5. single barrel, single-shot.

All of these guns are built in all conventional gauges and chokes. The single-shots are usually the least expensive (except for fancy trap guns) while the double-barrel side-by-sides and the over-and-unders, which involve a lot of hand fitting, top the scale. The pumps and autoloaders fall between the two in price. Most of these guns will shoot very well. In this respect, a high-

The five basic types of shotgun actions (all Winchesters, in this case): Top, a side-by-side double barrel; next, an over-and-under; center, a pump or slide action; next, a gas-operated autoloader, commonly termed "automatic"; bottom, an exposed hammer single-shot. The top four guns all have ventilated ribs. The over-and-under is a trap model, with a Monte Carlo stock.

113

priced shotgun has no great advantage to the buyer. On the other hand, you can rest assured that a finely made gun will perform reliably under all circumstances and probably have better balance. And, of course, there is pride of ownership to consider.

Requiring far less metal than others in their construction, single-shot shotguns are light in weight. Some weigh as little as 4½ pounds in a 20-gauge and from 5 to 5½ pounds in a 12-gauge. I won't need to remind anyone who has fired a high-base shell in an ultra-light shooting iron that they kick unmercifully. So if you have been thinking of giving your young son or daughter one of these ultra-light guns as a birthday or Christmas present . . . don't!

A single-shot break-open shotgun is a nice first gun for a boy or girl if you can find a 20-gauge weighing from 5½ to 6 pounds. If not, settle for a .410. The single-shot is the safest of all shotguns. It is easy to load and unload and is a fine builder of good shooting habits, for the young shooter must make his first shot count.

Pump guns have the advantage of holding more than one shell. Most of them, if unplugged, can be loaded with five or six shells. They are quite reliable in operation and handle reloaded shells fairly well. It takes some time to acquire the necessary skill to operate the slide action properly and to be able to shoot the second shot with speed and accuracy. To do so readily, you should grip the fore-end firmly and exert a backward pull on it before the first shot is fired. Some models require a slight forward movement of the fore-end first, to unlock the breech mechanism, before the sliding motion can be started back. With these, if your left hand has a firm grip, the recoil will drive the gun back far enough to unlock the action, and with the pull you are already exerting, the fore-end will instantly slide back. Thereafter, slide the fore-end forward and the next shot is ready to be fired.

On some pump guns the trigger must be released when you push the forearm forward. If it is not, the gun will fire again as soon as the action is fully closed. I have heard people say that they can fire an accurate second shot by holding the trigger down, but I have yet to see it done. Even George Neary, one of the fastest shots I have ever seen with a pump gun, who can kill a pigeon six feet off the ground and hit it with a second shot before it falls, lets go of the trigger for a fraction of a second. Most late model pumps have an interrupter and cannot be fired a second time unless the trigger is released.

I have seen exceptionally fine shooting done with pump guns, but I know from first-hand experience that anyone who thinks he can master a pump overnight simply doesn't know the facts of the matter. It takes patience and a lot of practice to be able to handle a pump gun well.

Automatics shoot from two to five shells without reloading, depending on their make. The modern auto-loader is very reliable and will work well with conventional factory-loaded shells if kept in good operating condition.

However, some owners of automatics neglect to clean their guns properly, or over-oil them, either of which will cause "hang-ups" or malfunctions. Many models have to be adjusted to handle different loads, such as low base, high base or magnum. Remember always to set them for the load you will be using. With a heavy setting and a light load, your gun may hang up, and if a heavy load is fired with the light load setting, you may damage the gun's action. It is good practice, therefore, to adjust the gun for the type of shell you expect to use on a hunting trip and take along only that shell. All guns come with instructions. Read them and follow them religiously and you'll have only a minimum of trouble. However, no matter what brand of automatic you purchase, it will, on occasion, hang up on you.

Double-barrel shotguns, both side-by-sides and over-and-unders, are probably the most reliable and safest of all, since they are actually two single-shots joined together in the same frame. These guns, with their two barrels, can also give you the advantage of different chokes — an open barrel for your first shot and a more tightly choked one for the second. The double-barrel side-by-sides are the easiest to load and unload. Most of them have an automatic safety device that engages the moment you open the gun. Therefore, when closed, the safety button will already be in the "safe" position.

Side-by-sides normally come with two triggers, the front one firing the right barrel and the rear one firing the left. However, some doubles are equipped or fitted with either a selective or a nonselective single trigger. A selective single trigger allows you to choose the barrel you wish to fire first. A nonselective single-trigger gun fires the right barrel first. In either case, a second trigger pull fires the second barrel.

116

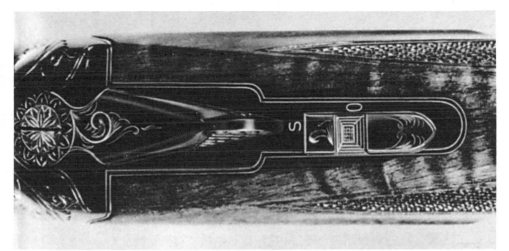

The position of the selector button for single triggers varies, but a common system is to combine this function with the safety, as on the Winchester Model 101 above. With the safety pushed to the left, as shown, the more tightly choked "over" barrel will be fired first.

Over-and-unders have most of the characteristics of side-by-sides, with double or single triggers, selective or nonselective. (The nonselective single trigger fires the lower barrel first.) One of the main advantages of the over-and-under is the single sighting plane it provides along the top of its upper barrel. It can be lined up just as a single barrel pump or automatic and provides the same "sight picture" so that one who has been shooting a pump or automatic will have no difficulty in making the change. Also, you have a somewhat better grip with your left hand. On incoming birds, providing you shoot with both eyes open, you can gauge your lead easier than with a side-by-side. A slight disadvantage is that, in order to load the bottom barrel, you must break the gun farther than you do to load a side-by-side. This can be cumbersome in a tank-type duck blind, although it can be overcome to a degree by holding the gun on its side when you break it.

If you buy a double-barrel shotgun, either side-by-side or over-and-under, it is wise to get one of good quality. Otherwise, you are usually better off purchasing a pump or an automatic. The average shooter usually begins with a less expensive gun, a single-barrel pump or an automatic. Later, he may graduate to a double-barrel gun to obtain the advantage of lighter weight, better balance and two barrels. The latter gives him the option of two different chokes. If the new gun has a single trigger, the shooter who is accustomed to a pump or automatic, will have no difficulty in adjusting. Why, then, even consider a double trigger? Because the double trigger is more reliable and the second shot can be gotten off faster. Also, because, if the need arises, the selection of one barrel over the other is easier and quicker.

Double triggers are more reliable because, having less complicated mechanisms, they will function better than the intricate construction to be found in single triggers, especially a selective one. Indeed, after all my years in the gun business, I know of very few single triggers I can trust, and sometimes even these can let you down. All single triggers should be cleaned yearly by a competent gunsmith to assure reliable functioning.

The advantage of being able to select your first barrel with a selective single trigger gun may also be questioned. There are moves to be made which may not be worthwhile, especially where the selection must be made by means of the safety catch. Suppose you are watching an incoming duck. You are in the ready position with the safety off. You decide the duck will be too far out to shoot with your open barrel so you wish to

118

switch. To do so you will have to pull the safety back, push it to the left and then forward again. These moves take too much time. Even with the selector on the trigger body in front of the trigger, you will need an extra move. And if your hand is gloved, it is even more trouble. Since there is usually only a 10 to 15 percent difference between the patterns of your barrels the advantage of selection may not offset the time lost in making it.

In the field, most of your shots are at going-away birds where, if you miss with the first, you will want the second to reach out further. Here, when shooting a gun with a single selective trigger, I set the selector to fire the more open barrel first and leave it there. Under most field conditions, therefore, a single selective trigger has little advantage over a nonselective one since the latter always fires the open barrel first.

Shooting doubles on the skeet field is when the selector comes into its own. On these stands there is an advantage in shooting the tighter barrel at the outgoing target and the more open one at the incomer, provided the barrels of your skeet gun are bored differently.

Certain kinds of single trigger offer yet another problem. After pulling the trigger for the first shot, you must let go and pull again for the second. Although recoil usually accomplishes this, people sometimes freeze on a trigger after the first shot, and block it. The second shot does not go off because the trigger was not released. The shooter, not realizing what happened, takes the gun from his shoulder to determine the trouble. Experimenting, he pulls the trigger again. This time, having released the trigger after the first shot, the gun fires. You can visualize what might happen to others

119

nearby, and the recoil could easily injure him. Just such an accident did occur to a friend of mine. The recoil drove the butt of the gun into his solar plexus, to his great discomfort and also the concern of his companions. Luckily, he broke no ribs nor did he hit any of us. The lesson to be had from this is that if your second barrel does not fire, unload the gun and try it empty, or if the gun needs the recoil from the first live shot to activate the trigger for the second, shoot it from your shoulder.

Single triggers should be avoided in 12-gauge magnum and 10-gauge guns. The recoil from their loads is excessive and the shock to the trigger mechanism soon throws it out of order.

There is, of course, no problem in selecting barrels with a double trigger gun. Normally you pull the front trigger first, which fires the right barrel in a side-by-side and the lower barrel of an over-and under. These are the more open barrels. Instantly, your finger slides back to the rear trigger and in this move the motion of the recoiling gun will help. The double-trigger routine is easy to learn. Many of my students shoot these guns and they master the trick with no special difficulty.

Incidentally, stocks with a straight grip are preferred for double triggers since your hold is more flexible and this permits you to go from trigger to trigger with greater ease. Sometimes, when pulling the back trigger of a double-barrel gun, your trigger finger will bruise itself against the front trigger. Wearing a glove or a band-aid will help. Many of the better quality double guns come with hinged front triggers which move forward and "give" when the trigger finger pushes against them.

120

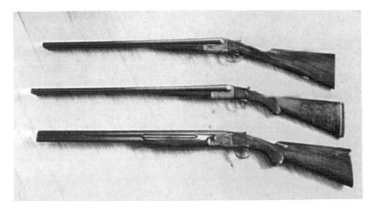

The three basic stock forms: straight, semi-pistol grip, and full-pistol grip. Double triggers and the classic English "straight hand" stock go well together.

Should you wish to use the second or tighter barrel first, it is easy enough to pull the rear trigger. In this case, your move to the front trigger will be less natural, but with practice you should have no trouble. (Three-time world champion Dr. Lumnitzer shot this way with great speed and accuracy. His only reason for doing so was that he learned it as a child, probably because at that time he could not reach the front trigger.)

The weight of trigger pull is partly a personal matter, but in general, from 3½ to 4 pounds is about right. The rear trigger of doubles is usually adjusted a trifle heavier than the front one, to insure against unintentional firing, and in any case "hair triggers" of less than 3½ pounds should be avoided. Trigger weights can be adjusted by a competent gunsmith, but work on single triggers comes high, and it is generally unwise to buy a second-hand single-trigger double if there is any question about the reliability of its functioning.

Do not let this discussion of triggers lead you to give them undue emphasis. They are important, but so are other parts, and they should not be your primary concern in choosing a gun. Indeed, the first thing to decide when you are ready to buy a shotgun is how it will chiefly be used — for general hunting in the field, for waterfowl shooting or for competitive shooting, such as skeet or trap. Unfortunately, there is no one gun that will do everything best.

WEIGHT

If you do a considerable amount of walking while hunting, you should purchase as light a gun as you can shoot comfortably. A tired hunter never shoots well. This is especially true of women and children. There is nothing worse than to burden a youngster with a gun which is already too heavy at the beginning of a hunt, let alone after carrying it around for four or five hours. The answer is a 20-gauge shotgun weighing between 5½ and 6½ pounds. It is a misconception that a 20-gauge gun has less recoil than a 12-gauge, for the recoil is entirely dependent on the weight of the gun and the load you shoot in it. For example, if you shoot a light 20-gauge gun with a high-base shell, it will have approximately the same recoil as a 12-gauge gun weighing from 1 to 1½ pounds more and shooting a light load. However, the ease with which a 20-gauge gun can be carried and handled is a considerable advantage.

Even for the experienced hunter a light gun has its advantages in the field. Twelve-gauge guns should not exceed 7 pounds for upland hunting. Chokes will depend upon the range at which you shoot and the type of load to be used. In general, a single-barrel pump or automatic with a Modified choke or a double-barrel gun with Improved-Cylinder and Modified chokes are the most useful for hunting in the field. Occasionally, if you go brush hunting, where the shooting is at ranges of thirty yards or less, a gun with open-bored barrels, such as Skeet or Improved-Cylinder, will do a better job.

If you hunt ducks and geese, a heavier gun is in order. You will probably use maximum loads and have to carry the gun only to and from the blind and when picking up downed birds. Best suited for waterfowl shooting are 12-gauge guns weighing at least 7½ pounds or 20-gauge guns weighing 6½ pounds or more and chambered for three-inch magnum shells. Single-barrel guns like automatics and pumps should be full-choked, while the doubles should be Modified and Full.

BARREL LENGTH

Barrels for field guns usually are from 25 to 30 inches in length. It should be noted, however, that length of barrel has practically no influence on the shooting performance of a gun since the useful power of the explosion is expended in the first 25 inches. Therefore, in selecting the barrel length for a field gun, your first consideration should be the gun's balance.

Basically, a shotgun should balance approximately 2¾ inches in front of the breech end of the barrel. However, this is only a crude yardstick, for balance is really a personal matter — the feel of a gun in your hands and when mounted. What feels right to one may not to another, just as of two golfers, one may prefer a D2 swing weight and the other, D4. The feel of the gun to

123

you is the important point and this will depend not only on your build and strength, but also on how you hold the gun. The more gun weight you place between your hands and your body, the better it will usually feel. This is an area where good gun makers excel and it is one reason why you pay more for a fine hand-made gun.

A 12-gauge gun, with its heavier frame and stock, will usually balance better with a 28-inch barrel, while a 20-gauge gun may give a better feel with a 26-inch barrel. A short-barreled gun in the hands of a large man looks out of proportion. The long stock, needed to accommodate his build, accentuates the shortness of the barrel, and the longer stock requires a longer barrel anyway in order to balance the gun. If your hunting is done mostly in dense cover where fast shooting is required, a 25- or 26-inch barrel will generally handle more easily.

A 30-inch barrel is preferred by most duck hunters as it gives them a longer sighting plane and less muzzle blast from the high-based shells that are so often used in this shooting. Twelve-gauge magnums should have barrels no less than 32 inches in length, except on pumps and automatics where the longer breech makes up the difference between face and muzzle. The blast from magnum shells can be very uncomfortable.

RIBS

In addition to a choice of barrel length in selecting a gun, you will have an option with respect to the rib. the metal strip which runs along the top of the barrel on a single-barrel gun or an over-and-under, and between the barrels of a side-by-side. The rib is necessary

124

on a side-by-side to help hold the two barrels together. Repeating guns come with or without ribs.

Ribs give you a better sighting plane to guide your vision over the barrel to the target. Generally speaking, ribs come in two categories: solid and ventilated. The solid rib is attached to the barrel for its full length, while the ventilated one is mounted on pillars so air can circulate under it and keep it cool. Ventilation is particularly important for trap shooting. A trap gun will heat up rapidly from continued fast firing, and without ventilation the rib may develop a heat wave, forming a mirage through which the view of the target will be distorted.

However, while ventilated ribs have become very popular on field guns in recent years they really serve no practical purpose for the everyday shooter. They are harder to clean, easier to dent, and they loosen up more readily than do the solid ones even though they may add a little less weight to a gun.

There are several types of ribs — wide ones, narrow ones and some that are wedge-shaped (wider at the breech than at the muzzle). Also, a cross-section view from the rear will show you flat, hollow and U-shaped ribs. The merits of each are frequently argued but the subject will probably never be resolved to everyone's satisfaction. To me, a satisfactory rib is one that is straight and has no glare on top, but I believe that anyone can easily learn to feel at home with the rib which comes with his gun.

A rib on an automatic is of questionable value because most of these guns come with a ramp sight, and when you sight down the top of the receiver to the bead on the ramp, the space between, where the rib would be, is not visible. Ribs on automatics only tend to increase the weight of the gun, making an already heavy barrel heavier.

SIGHTS

Most guns come from the manufacturer with a metal bead for the front sight. Frequently these are too small and hard to see, but they can be replaced at a nominal price by different custom sights. Many of these come in either white or red and in various sizes. The ones enclosed in a metal base do not break as easily as those which are made entirely from ivory, bone or plastic.

Later additions to the shotgun-sight family are those made of colored lucite, usually red. These have a certain luminosity and can be seen better than most other sights, especially when the visibility is poor. They are quite helpful to those with poor eyesight but for my taste they are a bit large and look ungainly on the end of a barrel.

Center beads, or middle sights, can be mounted on ribs about 14 to 15 inches from the breech end of the barrel. These sights, which are smaller than the ones in front, will warn you against faulty handling of the gun. When the gun is held correctly while sighting down the barrel, the middle bead blends into the larger one and all you see is the front sight (unless you intentionally wish the gun to shoot high, as in trapshooting). If, however, you see the two sights separately, to one side or the other, you can be sure the gun is tilted (canted).

126

EXTRA BARRELS

When buying a gun, you might also consider an extra barrel or set of barrels. With the right combination, you will have a single gun that can be used for all types of game shooting under almost any circumstances.

If you get a double-barrel gun with one set of barrels bored skeet and skeet, and the other modified and full, you will have a good upland game gun as well as a very desirable duck gun. You can also use it for both skeet and trap shooting. If you are not a skeet shooter but do a lot of bird hunting over a dog, you may want your more open set of barrels bored improved-cylinder and modified.

Some makers can fit your gun with an extra set of barrels later, but it is time-consuming work and can be expensive. It is better to buy a double barrel gun with two sets of barrels in the first place, if the option is available. It is also advisable to choose sets of barrels with identical lengths or ones varying not more than two inches. While there is not much difference in weight, the balance of a gun changes quite noticeably when barrels vary as much as three or four inches in length.

The most desirable combination of two barrels for pump or automatic shotguns are chokes of improved cylinder and full.

VARIABLE CHOKE DEVICES

While extra barrels are the best solution if you are seeking an all-around shotgun, variable choking devices can be installed on guns with a single barrel. These have also been made for double-barrel guns, but with little acceptance by the shooting fraternity.

Many choke-changing barrel attachments have been invented and marketed during the last twenty-five years. They can be classified in two groups — those that can be adjusted by a simple twist of the wrist and those which use different interchangeable choke tubes. The hand-adjustable ones are the more practical for hunting as you do not have to carry a wrench and extra tubes in order to change the choke. Also, the adjustment from one choke to another can be made within seconds. However, anyone who has one of these devices at the end of his shotgun barrel should pattern it with the different settings, for the markings on them, designating certain chokes, are only guides. There is no certainty that your gun will shoot a truly full-choke pattern at the full-choke setting. The chances are that you will have to move the regulator a notch or two one way or the other to achieve the desired result.

For competitive shooting, the choke devices with interchangeable tubes are the most popular. There is little chance of accidentally setting the choke at the wrong constriction when using one of these and they also have an increased braking action to cut down recoil more than the hand adjusted types. A fault with choke systems having a muzzle brake is that they expel an excessive side blast which, to say the least, is annoying to a hunting partner or shooting opponent close by when you fire.

MAGNUMS

If you can take the punishment and want to reach out to the extreme limits of shotgun shooting, the 12-

128

gauge magnum and, where permitted, 10-gauge magnum will prove useful. These guns will extend your killing range by approximately 25 yards — not more. shots claimed at 100 yards with these guns are either accidental or, more often, mistakes in judging distance. Maximum effective range at which an exceptionally good shot can score consistently, is not more than 70 yards. However, if you think this isn't a long shot, buy a toy balloon and tie it to a 70-yard string. Let it rise straight up on a calm day and by the time the string has been completely payed out, you will swear the balloon is more than 70 yards up. These guns should be used only with large shot (4 or 2). Otherwise, they will only cripple many birds, as small shot loses its velocity quickly and lacks sufficient penetration at the extreme ranges for which the guns are designed. The 12-gauge magnum shotgun should weigh not less than 8 pounds; the 10-gauge not less than 9. Even then, they are mean to use unless the shooter happens to be immune to recoil.

Before closing this chapter, let me offer a word of advice about secondhand guns. You can save money buying one, but you are wise to deal only with a reliable dealer or in consultation with a gunsmith who can verify that the gun is in sound, safe condition. Never buy guns with Damascus, twist, or laminated steel barrels. they are dangerous, for they do not have the strength to handle modern ammunition. When buying a secondhand gun, check that the chamber length will handle the type of shell you expect to use — no 3-inch magnums in 2¾-inch chambers. Some imported guns are chambered for 2½-inch shells (marked 65mm.) only; do not shoot any 2¾-inch loads in these without having the chambers lengthened. Also, some are proofed for only

129

low base shells, and no high-base loads should ever be shot in these.

Imported guns, especially, should be bought only from reputable dealers who will stand behind them. Since World War II tens of thousands of foreign shotguns have been imported, some of which are not worth the shipping charges. Others, however, are well worth the price asked for them.

There is only one remaining type of shotgun which I have not discussed, simply because it does not merit serious mention. This is the bolt action repeater which looks like a rifle and handles like one. These monstrosities have only one advantage: they are cheap.

CHAPTER **10**

Guns for Competitive Shooting

The novice shotgunner who wishes to go in for competitive shooting (skeet or trap) should be aware of the basic fact that all shooters are handicapped by both noise and recoil, whether or not they realize it. Both produce a mental and physical shock which must be withstood each time the trigger is pulled. The less the shooter is bothered by these external influences — the more they can be reduced — the easier it will be to concentrate on the shot at hand.

Cutting down on the noise is comparatively easy. Earplugs or muff-type protectors are the answer, as discussed on page 148. Reducing recoil can be accomplished in several ways. The simplest is to choose a heavy gun, particularly for trap shooting, or use a gas-operated semiautomatic. Recoil-reducing devices can also be installed, some being mounted on the muzzle while others fit into the stock. (Muzzle devices, however, are rarely fitted to trap guns; they create an excessive side blast and many trap fields do not allow them.) My experience with stock devices has been limited, but among those who have used them, I find that opinion as to their merits is pretty much divided. Some of these devices have an extra piece of stock cushioned by a hydraulic cylinder, while others use a spring-loaded weight that swings back and forth inside the stock when the gun is fired.

Rubber recoil pads are used frequently, and while they cannot actually reduce the kick itself, they will cushion it to some extent, especially if the pad is cushioned by air spaces or "ventilated." These pads also can be used to change the length of a stock or the pitch of a gun. When a stock is shortened, it is common practice to install a pad because the original butt plate is usually curved and very difficult to refit. Many people like to glue a strip of leather or smooth plastic material to the butt of a rubber pad (using rubber cement that will not harden) to prevent it from sticking to their clothing when the gun is mounted. This is very desirable for hunting and International skeet, where fast and accurate gun mounting is essential.

A second type which should be mentioned is the adjustable recoil pad, widely used by trap shooters. This consists of a serrated metal plate with a separate rubber pad which is also mounted on a serrated metal plate.

The two plates face each other, the first being permanently affixed to the stock, while the one with the rubber pad can be adjusted up or down to change the drop of the gun at its heel. These pads come with either a straight or curved rubber piece and can be quite helpful to a trap shooter. Once the adjustment is made, it should not be changed unless absolutely necessary because frequent changes in stock measurements can only lead to confusion.

I come now to the actual selection of a gun for competition. For 12-gauge skeet I would purchase a good quality gas-operated autoloader because of its minimal recoil. My second choice would be a double-barrel over-and-under or side-by-side. These guns should weigh not less than seven and a half pounds, have front and center bead sights, and all barrels should be choked Skeet No. 1 and Skeet No. 2. The No. 2 barrel is a little tighter than the other and is used on the outgoing targets when shooting doubles. If it is not too heavy such a gun can also be used for dove, quail or any brush hunting.

Skeet guns should be patterned at 25 yards, as this is usually the maximum range at which you will shoot a skeet target. At that distance they should put 90 percent of the shot charge in a thirty-inch circle with even distribution, which is essential.

Competitive skeet is also shot with 20, 28, and .410 gauge guns. Some of the 12's are available with extra barrels in these smaller gauges. The interchangeable barrels are weighted and balanced to give the same feel as the 12-gauge gun. While in most cases these sets are quite expensive, they are usually preferred by serious

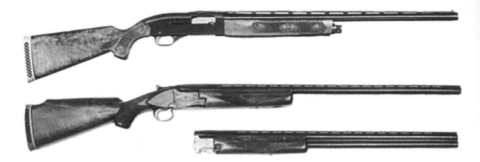

Specialized skeet and trap guns represent opposite extremes—skeet guns should be short barreled and open choked, traps guns just the opposite. Automatics like the top gun are fine for skeet, but I prefer the over-and-under action in a trap gun. Some over-and-unders are available with interchangeable single barrels, like that shown on the Winchester 101.

competitors. When separate guns are purchased for the different gauges, the 20, 28, and .410 will be lighter than the 12 and should have weights attached to their barrels to give them the same balance and feel as the 12. These also should have ventilated ribs.

For trap shooting, my first choice is a 12-gauge over-and-under with a 30- to 32-inch barrel, ventilated rib, and front and center bead sights. It should weigh not less than seven and a half pounds. The advantage of this gun is that it can be used for either American or International trap (when two shots are permitted) and, of course, for shooting doubles. Last, but not least, it will make a good duck gun.

Trap targets are shot at while rising, so your gun should shoot high to give you a built-in lead. This allows you to see the target when you pull the trigger, and not cover it up when firing. Seeing the target is particularly important in International trap, which permits a quick second shot should you miss with the first; you can see immediately whether the second shot is needed.

134

There are several ways to make a gun shoot high. One is to raise the comb, which pushes the butt down and the barrel up so that some of the rib becomes visible to your sighting eye. Another method is to use the center bead to give you a figure-eight sighting picture by placing the front bead on top of it. While this will raise the point of impact, a disadvantage is that different lighting tends to change the amount of rib you see.

Probably the best way to make your gun shoot high is to build it in by adjusting the relationship between rib and barrel. The higher the rib is at the breech and the lower at the muzzle, the more the barrel will be tilted up and the higher the gun will shoot. You can line up your sight the same way each time without having to rely on a personalized tilting of the barrel.

Usually a trap gun puts approximately two-thirds of its pattern above the target, which at forty yards means an elevation of about ten inches.

The chokes for this gun should be modified or improved modified, and full. While these chokes are usually adequate for American trap, you need them tighter for the International game. There, the first barrel should put not less than 70 percent of the shot charge in a thirty-inch circle at forty yards, and the second between 75 and 80 percent. These tighter chokes are needed because in International trap the targets travel eighty yards or more, compared to only fifty in American trap.

Triggers for all trap guns should be either double or selective single so the full choke barrel may be fired first when needed, as in handicap trap.

Some of these guns come with an interchangeable single-barrel for American trap shooting. The advantage

here is that the single-barrel does not offer as much surface to the wind as does a regular over-and-under. Long
barrels are desirable on trap guns. Their longer sighting
plane is helpful and their added weight keeps you
swinging.

Automatics are not welcome on trap fields for serious competition, although they have been used at times
by some great champions. They are prone to malfunction and unless fitted with a special shell catcher, they
throw the empty shells in front of the shooter on the
right, to which most people object.

There are other types of guns, of course, that can
be used successfully for clay target shooting, but if you
choose one of those described above, I am sure you will
have a satisfactory gun for the purpose. No matter what
your gun, my advice to the beginner is that which I
received many years ago from Olympic champion Halasi : "Never look at the score board but concentrate
only on the target coming up. If you always hit the next
target, you will win the race." Remember too, the sharp-
er your physical and mental condition, the more you
conserve your strength, the better you will shoot and
the longer you will last.

CHAPTER **11**

Gun Fitting

I have spent many years fitting guns to people and sometimes I wonder just how important this is to the shooter. I have witnessed some remarkable shooting by men with guns that I knew did not fit. One of our most prominent skeet shooters, who has racked up many championships, uses a gun with a ridiculously short stock. For years I used a pair of guns that did not fit at all, but I won lots of trophies with them. And in 1930, I saw Mark Arie win the World Trapshooting Championship in Rome with a beaten-up old pump gun that had certainly not been fitted by an expert. But these examples only serve to show that you can shoot almost any gun once you are acquainted with it. Again, one of the finest European game shots, my friend Count Laszlo Szapáry, uses a set of ordinary autoloaders on occasion and thinks nothing of shooting twenty-five high driven pheasants in succession. And another friend of mine, George Neary, after winning the championship in Barcelona in 1963, proceeded to shoot six pigeons consecutively, holding the gun at his hip.

Feats of this sort, and many similar ones, are only possible after long years of practice, and even these experts, when the chips are down and precision shooting is essential, prefer and use a properly fitted gun.

I have often heard it said that "the best gun I ever owned is that old double my grandfather gave me. I can still shoot it better than anything else." Of course he can; after twenty years together, he and the gun understand each other. His shooting style has adjusted to the gun, and no other gun, with different weight and balance, will feel right to him unless fitted to accommodate his build and way of shooting. The more advanced the shooter, the more ingrained his style, the greater his need to have his gun fitted. On the other hand, with a beginner, a run-of-mill gun with normal measurements will fit in most cases, needing only the length of stock to be adjusted. The novice has developed no hard-boned habits, but the older hand, with a well-established way of shooting, should always have his guns fitted.

The basic principle of shotgun shooting is that you shoot where you look, and when it is properly lined up, you look with the gun. The reason for fitting is to help you start looking with the gun the instant the butt hits your shoulder. The gun must be so adjusted to your build and style of shooting that you find yourself looking down the rib and at the target the moment the gun is mounted. This is what fitting is all about: to make it easy for you, without any loss of time, to coordinate your line of vision from eye to target with the line in which the shot will fly from muzzle to target. You may learn to shoot well with "any old gun," but you will do it better and with much more ease using a gun that was fitted to you, which you do not have to fight and consciously position. The well-fitted gun will always show its worth, especially when fast shooting is essential.

Perhaps you will better understand the importance of a good fit if we take a separate look at each measurement used by the fitter. There are five of them, listed below, and three are shown in the accompanying illustration.

1. Length of stock
2. Drop at comb
3. Drop at heel
4. Cast-off (or "on" for a left-handed shooter)
5. Pitch

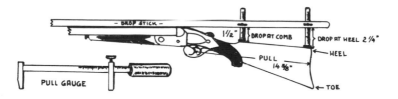

The handiest way to check gun measurements is with a drop stick and a pull gauge, as shown above. As a practical matter, however, you can place the inverted gun on a table and take off the same measurements with an ordinary yard-stick or a long ruler. The measurements in the diagram are typical factory dimension.

The *length of stock* measurement is from the center of the trigger (the front trigger with a double-trigger gun) to the middle of the butt. This measurement happens to be the least important of all because, if the others are right, the length of stock can vary plus or minus half an inch and you will still be able to shoot the gun with no great difficulty.

For general field use and skeet shooting, the stock should be as short as possible. The more gun you can place between body and hands, the better you can control it. With too much gun beyond your reach, its weight tends to take over your swing.

The question, then, is how short is short, and this depends on the right-hand hold. When the gun is mounted, there should be a gap of at least three-quarters of an inch between the shooter's nose and his nearest finger in line with it. The recoil drives the gun back into the shoulder about half an inch, so with a three-quarter-inch gap you should not punch yourself in the nose every time you pull the trigger.

Even after a gun has been fitted, if your hold on the grip is too loose, your middle finger may get bruised. An easy remedy for this is to slip a soft rubber ball, a so-called finger guard, on the trigger guard.

A common method of measuring stock length is to hold the gun upright with the butt in the crook of your elbow, your hand on the grip and your finger on the trigger. This method is not very accurate and should not be relied upon.

The second and third measurements, *drop at comb* and *drop at heel,* are taken for different reasons, but they are dependent on each other, and when one is al-

140

tered, the other may also need some change to give a proper fit.

The *drop at comb* regulates the height at which your line of vision begins — in other words, the height of your eye. When the gun is mounted in the correct shooting position, with shoulder hunched and head tilted forward, the stock will come up under the cheekbone and no higher; but this may place the sighting plane of a new gun above or below your line of vision. To bring them together, to coordinate your line of vision with the sighting plane of the gun, the comb will need to be raised or lowered. A gunfitter needs the correct drop at comb measurement to make the necessary adjustment.

The position of the heel should be such that the entire butt can rest against your shoulder, so as to spread the recoil over as wide a surface as possible and not concentrate it in a restricted area. The *drop at heel* measurement has much to do with this, because, if the

Positioning the stock too high on the shoulder, a result of poor gun mounting or too straight a stock, often results in bruises and erratic shooting.

heel shows above the shoulder, the butt is too high, and, similarly, it may come up too low. The position of the butt is related to the height of the comb, for if the comb is raised, the heel will probably be too high, and vice versa. The reason, then, for taking the drop at heel measurement is to place the butt at the height required for all of it to rest against the shoulder; but this also requires the correct pitch, which will be explained in the paragraph after next.

Cast-off compensates for the lateral distance between eye and cheekbone, much as drop at comb does for the vertical distance. Cast-off is the diversion of the stock to the right, so that when the butt is placed against the shoulder, your aiming eye will look down a line drawn up the center of the rib. The degree of cast-off is the length of the horizontal distance from your eye to that center line. Most well-made guns come with

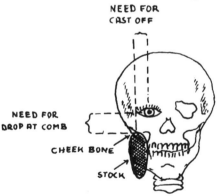

Cast-off is the amount of lateral deviation of the stock to the right that is required to permit the aiming eye to look down the center of the rib when the butt is placed properly against the shoulder. It serves to compensate for the lateral distance between eye and cheekbone, just as the drop at comb compensates for the vertical distance.

142

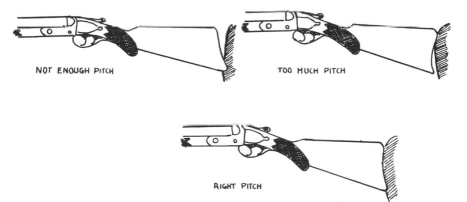

NOT ENOUGH PITCH

TOO MUCH PITCH

RIGHT PITCH

Pitch is the muzzle's deviation from a true vertical when the butt rests squarely on a true horizontal. In practice, however, pitch is the angle at which the butt rests against your shoulder, and it is correct only when the entire surface of the butt makes even contact.

a slight cast-off to start with, approximately one-quarter of an inch, and the toe is usually cast-off more than the heel, to allow the butt to follow the shoulder structure.

Pitch is the tilt at which the butt rests against your shoulder. This is most important to a good fit, though many shooters and some people in the profession do not realize it. Even though the drop at heel has been properly adjusted, the fit will be wrong unless the angle of the butt permits its entire surface to rest against the shoulder. If the angle is too sharp, so that only the toe hits the shoulder, you will soon be bruised by the recoil, since a pointed object hits harder than one with a flat surface; and if the angle is reversed, with the heel mostly against the shoulder, the gun will tend to slip up and the recoil will be felt on your cheekbone. In either case, the gun is apt to wobble and not come up twice in the same place. The proper pitch, of course, is that which places all of the butt against the shoulder.

143

Once the gun shoots right for you, don't change its measurements just because you miss a few shots. Misses are usually your own fault and should not be blamed on the gun. While details of gun-fit are of interest primarily to professionals, I believe that some knowledge of the art of gun-fitting will be helpful to all shooters, especially as they become more advanced in the sport. Shooting well is difficult enough as it is, without making it harder by shooting a poorly fitting gun.

CHAPTER **12**

Shooting
Accessories
and Clothes

Accessories should serve their purpose in a simple, easy way, with the emphasis on utility. I believe in traveling light on foot, and the more you can leave in the car, except shells, the better off you will be.

To carry shotgun shells in an automobile, use a leather pouch or a shell bag with a carrying strap that will hold no less than four boxes. In the field, I like to carry as few gadgets as possible and rely on a good hunting vest or coat with large enough pockets to accommodate fifty rounds. For use in a duck blind, a shell bag that is waterproof and can be placed on the floor of the blind or hung from a hook on the side is an advantage. While the new plastic shells have eliminated the problem of wet and swollen shells, it is still a nuisance to have the boxes get wet and fall apart, for if you are using more than one load, you must sort out the shells after the shoot.

Some hunters prefer shell belts, but I consider them too heavy, unless made of canvas, and excessively hot around the waist. It is also easy to lose shells from them. If, when in the field, you have to carry more shells than your pockets will hold, carry them in a shell bag. Just make sure the strap is over your left shoulder, leaving your right one free for the gun butt. Any kind of wrinkle, strap or even suspender can interfere with proper gun mounting. So when you shoot, use a belt to hold up your trousers or sling your right suspender over your left shoulder. And always button your hunting jacket, at least at the top, to avoid any wrinkle that might hamper you in mounting the gun.

When shells are carried loose in your pockets or in a shell bag, shake them well before starting to shoot. The heavier weight of the shot in the shells will cause their loading ends to turn down and the brass ends to come up. In this position they will be easier to handle when loading. While discussing the chore of carrying ammunition, I would also like to make this suggestion. Always take along twice as many shells as you think you will need. Nothing is more frustrating than to run out of shells, and of course it always happens when the birds you seek are blackening the sky and close enough to catch with a butterfly net.

Duck straps are very useful, especially the harness type that won't slip off your shoulder when the around-the-chest strap is buckled. They leave both your hands free to carry your gun, decoys and shell pouch when you leave the blind. Small bird straps for doves, quail and partridge are becoming very popular, particularly for use in warm weather. These are made to hang from your belt and allow the birds to cool out quickly. Their only drawback is that your pants leg sometimes becomes bloody. This can be prevented, however, by hanging a piece of oilcloth or plastic from your belt under the strap.

A shooting glove on the left hand is sometimes very helpful. In heavy country, it can be held in front of you to separate branches and protect your gun while the gun shields your face. You can also use it to pick up game, to reach where you might not wish to with a naked hand, and to carry your gun in cold weather. I do not like to have my trigger hand covered, so in cold weather I make sure to have a good right-hand pocket with a hand-warmer in it.

Much as I believe in traveling light, I also believe

A left-hand glove can be very useful when going through heavy country. The gloved hand protects the gun while the gun shields your face, your trigger finger on the guard prevents twigs from touching the trigger, and the left hand is already at eye level, ready to grasp the fore-end instantly if a bird gets up.

in being prepared for emergencies. A good example of this was recently given me by my Mexican guide, Leo Peterson. I have hunted quail with him for several years and he always appears to carry nothing with him. This time my hunting companion returned to the car with a piece of cholla cactus caught in his hand. The spines were sticking out in all directions so he could not use his other hand to remove it. Leo promptly pulled an ordinary table fork from his shirt, slid it under the offending object with the tines between the cactus spines, and flipped it off – all in the day's work. I then asked Leo what else he carried and, after considerable prodding, he brought forth a razor blade and some Band-Aids. This was his snake-bite kit and, if necessary, he could use a shoelace for a tourniquet. When you think of it, a very simple and effective kit to carry.

When shooting skeet or trap, your ears should be protected. Earplugs are helpful, some more than others, but the earmuff types are better since they cover the ears and also the bones which conduct sound. When nothing else is available, use cotton or balled-up facial tissues.

Special shooting glasses are very practical, whether or not you need prescription lenses. These glasses are larger than reading glasses and will protect your eyes from any powder or other residue that may be flying around. The difficulty with regular glasses is that when your head is tilted forward in the shooting position, the upper part of the rims often interferes with your vision. Shooting glasses, however, have a large glass surface and, if properly fitted, they "ride high" so you look through the lens even with your head forward.

You can buy shooting glasses in an amber color or in shades of green or gray. On a sunny day I prefer the No. 2 green shade, which is a light green. If the visibility is poor, the amber color will give you excellent definition. These amber glasses are also useful when driving at night to cut down the glare of oncoming headlights.

A small compass, mounted on a waterproof match box, is an accessory that often comes in handy, especially when fog rolls in suddenly in strange country. This and a good pocket knife should be standard equipment. An insect repellent can give you much comfort in mosquito country. Perhaps the most important shooting accessory of all is the gun case. The so-called full-length cases are probably the most convenient, since shotguns carried in them do not have to be dismantled, but the rigid, hard-leather, leg-of-mutton and trunk-type cases give a gun far better protection. The most easily damaged part of a shotgun is its barrels. If it or they become dented or bent, you are in for a costly repair job. Sometimes they are irreparable. I have seen barrels that had been badly bent while lying on the back seat of a car in a full-length case. They had been sat on by a heavy man. A full-length case is all right if you are very careful of your gun while traveling to and from your hunts. But if you want to be completely free of damage worry, get a rigid case and assemble and disassemble your gun when taking it out or putting it in the case.

When the hunt is over, never place your gun on top of the car. If you aren't going to pack it away immediately, put it on the hood. Recently, one of my shooting partners drove off with his $3,000 Purdey on the roof of the car. He is still looking for it.

For many years I have considered game calls, and especially duck calls, to be among the greatest devices ever invented — for ducks. The average duck hunter does not know how to use them and not only will his calling be ineffective but he will probably scare the birds out of the county. Here again, learn from an expert or at least get an instruction record and practice with it. Some remarkable results can be achieved by one who knows, but the hunter who has not learned had better rely on his camouflage and decoys.

HUNTING CLOTHES

Clothes cannot make you a better shooter, but the right ones will add much pleasure to your hunting. If they don't suit terrain or weather, you may feel uncomfortable and not shoot well. You should never be conscious of clothes; they should just be a part of you.

When hunting migratory birds the less conspicuous you are the better. You are usually in a blind or other sheltered spot where you wait for them to fly within range. Camouflage clothing is best for this shooting, with dark-colored clothes next. The most important item is the hat, since it is visible for some distance. I have always preferred one with a wide, pliable brim all around, to conceal my face and to shield my eyes from the sun. Visor caps and deerstalker-type hats may look well on the mannequin in a store window but when the rain begins to trickle in under your collar, or the sun starts baking your neck to a nice beet color, you may have some second thoughts about that headpiece.

Few hunting jackets serve the purpose really satisfactorily, and none meets with everyone's approval. The jacket should be wind proof and have a collar narrow enough not to interfere with gun mounting, but with a tab to button up in cold weather. It should have large side pockets for shells, slanted so that when you kneel or bend forward, none will drop out. There should be no pocket on the right breast but one on the left, large enough to hold glasses and one or two other small articles. Stretch loops on each side are useful to carry shells with different loads. The game pocket behind should be blood-proof and ride high on your back so the game will not bounce around as you walk. There should be room enough to move freely and to wear a sweater underneath in cold weather.

Hunting pants are better and last longer with a canvas or nylon reinforcement in front, or plastic in thorny country. In heavy cover, plastic is the only material that will stand up and not get heavy or shrink when wet.

Tuck-in pants, while warmer than those that ride outside your shoes, are good in reedy country and where ticks and other bugs are apt to crawl up your legs. Wear your socks outside and rolled down to your shoe tops as added protection. I found this very helpful when hunting in Africa.

Lined pants are fine for cold weather, but if the lining is red, be sure it does not bleed when wet. A belt is preferable to suspenders and in a pinch can serve as dog leash or duck strap.

I have also found a scarf to be very useful on a cold or windy day. In extremely cold weather I like one long enough to tie over my hat, under my chin and around my coat collar.

A leather jacket is good, too, in cold weather — one with knitted cuffs and waistband, similar to those worn by motorcycle riders. When zipped up it will keep the warmth in, and when unzipped there will be plenty of ventilation to keep you cool. It gives ample room for movement and will not interfere with gun mounting. The lack of pockets can be overcome by wearing a combination shell and game carrier. This has a game pouch in back and two large side pockets for shells. It hangs on two straps that go over your shoulders cross-wise and is held together by a buckle in front. I use this carrier in either hot or cold weather since it can be worn over a T-shirt as well as heavy clothing.

In cold weather I prefer "layer" clothing rather than one big, warm jacket. It is easy then to strip down for walking, stowing the extra pieces in your game pocket, and when you stop you can put them on again as needed. Wet underwear can get pretty cold if you have to wait around for long.

When hunting residential game you are usually walking up, often with other hunters. As a precaution against being shot, you should wear something bright and eye-catching. Here, again, your hat is the most conspicuous, and either red, yellow or orange (like a highway vest) is the color to use. There seems to be no agreement as to which color is most visible, but play it safe anyway and wear one of them.

Shoes are a most important part of your hunting apparel, for if they do not fit you can be in for trouble. I always wear a pair that has been broken in, a pair that I have hiked in before, which I am sure won't bite.

I prefer shoes as light as possible but with a sole firm enough so that I do not feel each pebble stepped on. Big, heavy shoes are a handicap in country where they're not needed; you are only lifting added weight with each step. Shoes need to be cared for after the hunt, like your gun. They should be cleaned and treated with a leather preservative, applied in a warm, liquid form to be sure the leather will absorb it. Shoelaces should be checked and replaced before they break.

I like to wear two pairs of socks when hunting — thin cotton or cotton-and-nylon next to the skin and a heavy woolen pair outside. This gives both moisture absorption and cushioning at the same time.

CHAPTER **13**

Gun Care

To me, cleaning a gun is the only boring thing about shooting, but since it is also necessary, I believe in doing it in the easiest manner possible. In the first place, much work can be avoided if the gun is not abused. Use it for shooting only — not as a walking stick, or a block on which to bang the heads of game — and clean it promptly and thoroughly when the need arises.

Thanks to modern ammunition, guns today require little cleaning, and not much equipment is needed for the job. A cleaning rod is, of course, essential. My preference is a wooden one, or one of metal that is covered with plastic, as I do not like the sound of metal against metal in the barrels. Next, you need a jag with a serrated tip to screw on the end of the cleaning rod. Be sure that it will fit the gauge of your gun. A 12 gauge jag, holding a patch, will usually not fit a 20-gauge gun, and if it is forced through the barrel, the thin walls may be damaged. The jag should hold one or two patches with enough pressure against the barrel walls to clean them. Do not use jags with long necks and a hole through which to pull a patch. These usually come with cheap cleaning kits and are meant for rifles. Round flannel patches are the best, but again, be sure you have the right size so you do not need to force the rod through the barrel. In an emergency facial tissue or even newspaper may be used, but paper must be handled with care for it tends to wad up in a ball which may be difficult to push through the barrel. Remember always that the barrel walls are quite thin and all unnecessary strain on them should be avoided.

Though I do not usually recommend equipment by brand, there is one item that has proved so useful to me in cleaning a gun that I cannot refrain from mentioning it. This is the W. W. cleaner, which looks like an elongated, outsize pipe cleaner and comes in a case that might hold a fly rod. It will perform marvels with the least effort. Pushed through a barrel once or twice, its tough synthetic fibers will remove all grime and powder residue, and most of the time no additional cleaning is necessary. And when the cleaner itself gets too dirty, take it into the shower with you.

The oil you use plays a most important part in cleaning your gun. It should always be of the best quality. There are several excellent brands that will provide cleaning, lubrication and rust prevention, and also act as a solvent, all at the same time. My preference is one with a sperm oil base since this will adhere to the barrel walls and not run as easily as a thin oil. Also, I prefer an oil that comes in a pressurized spray can because, when sprayed into a barrel, the oil forms an even film over the entire wall. With an ordinary can, the patch you must use soaks up so much of the oil that the muzzle end often does not receive as much as the breech. Sprayed oil will penetrate to places that are difficult to reach with oil from a conventional can. A silicone cloth will complete your cleaning equipment.

Always take a gun apart before beginning to clean it, especially a side-by-side or an over-and-under, to avoid unnecessary strain on an opened gun. The barrel walls should be cleaned from the breech end and the barrel should be hand-held in the process. If a vise is used, padded inserts should be applied and the barrel clamped in with modest force only and at its thickest end. Never clamp a barrel near its center as the force may be too great for the thin walls.

The easiest way to clean a barrel, as mentioned before, is to push a W. W. cleaner through once or twice and then look for leading or other residue. To inspect the barrel, turn it toward a bright light and position it so you have a cone of light through the inside. Gently move the barrel up and down so the cone will travel through the barrel; then rotate and inspect all sides. Now do the same thing from the muzzle end. This procedure will show you the slightest leading and also any pitting or denting of the barrel.

If you find no residue, spray one or two short

I find the pipe-cleaner-like W.W. type of rod at left especially handy and adequate for almost all cleaning duty. Leading will sometimes require use of a spiral or bronze wire brush like those in the middle, however.

bursts of oil through the barrel. Do the same inside the breech and trigger guard and wipe off excess oil with a patch. The outside of the gun should now be wiped with a silicone cloth to remove all dirt and fingerprints. The cloth will also leave a protective film on the steel parts and the stock, which will harden in time to a lustrous finish and give added protection against rusting or wearing of the stock. Silicone should not be used on oily surfaces.

Always use oil sparingly; too much not only does not help, but if it seeps into the stock it may soften the wood. Also, some oils harden in the action, which can cause triggers and other parts to malfunction.

157

If you use a conventional cleaning rod, spray oil into barrel first, or run an oil patch through. Leave the oil there for a few minutes and then push dry patches through until they come out clean. After that, inspect for any fouling in the barrel.

When lead or other residue is found, it should be cleaned out immediately, since any substance trapped beneath might pit the barrel. Now a solvent should be used, followed by a wire brush to take out the fouling. Never use wire brushes in a dry barrel. I prefer brushes of copper or bronze as steel brushes are too harsh for barrel walls. As a last resort, a very fine steel wool may be used, but this is better left to a competent gunsmith. After removing the residue, wipe the barrels clean and finish off the gun as you would if no wire brush had been used.

Always be sure your barrels are clean and free of grease and oil before you go shooting. With the tight sealing wads now used in shells, even excessive oil or grease has been known to bulge barrels.

If your gun has gotten wet, in the rain or otherwise, it should receive a meticulous cleaning. Use the spray can first and then go to work. When you hunt near salt water, take a spray can with you and use it lavishly on the outside of your gun before you start. Except for blood, nothing will rust a gun faster than exposure to salt water or even salt-laden air. If you get blood on your gun, wipe it off immediately and clean thoroughly as soon as possible.

Never put a wet gun in a case as this is certain to start rust, and be sure the case is dry before leaving a gun in it. When you buy a full-length case, get one with a full-length zipper so it can be opened up to dry out if necessary. Before storing your gun in a case for any extended period, a film of good quality gun grease should be applied, both inside and out, but be sure this is removed before again using the gun. An excellent protection for extended storage is V. P. I. paper, which is chemically treated to emit gases that will prevent rusting in confined areas, such as gun cases and cabinets. The effect of this paper will usually last for about six months. Never plug barrels when storing guns, since rust forms more easily in unventilated areas. Nor should you expect the bluing on your gun to protect the outside finish, for actually bluing is itself a rusting process.

Guns stored in a humid climate need special attention. Even when put away well greased they tend to rust or corrode within a few months; they need constant care. A friend in a humid area tells me that he puts his guns down in hard cases with little jars of activated alumina to absorb the dampness. From time to time he removes the jars and heats them to drive off the moisture. He has found this to be very helpful.

Before putting your gun away for any length of time, release the hammer spring by pulling the trigger. Be sure the gun is loaded with a snap shell or a dry empty cartridge, since pulling the trigger on an empty chamber may break the firing pin if it meets no resistance.

If you have trouble with the trigger mechanism of your shotgun, don't just wait for it to go away. It won't. Triggers are much like the brakes on your car — they are highly dangerous unless in excellent working order!

Finally, your shotguns should be cleaned thoroughly at the end of the hunting season by a competent gun-smith. There are parts the layman cannot and should not reach. This is especially true of double-barrel side-by-sides and over-and-under guns. Moisture steals into the actions and sooner or later will start a rusting process. The most sensitive parts in the actions of these guns are the springs and, if broken, they must be replaced. Some are hand-made and fitted, and are very costly. Also, any leading of the barrels or collection of plastic residue in them can be removed more easily and thoroughly by a gunsmith.

160